Jay Quinn

The Mentor
A Memoir of Friendship and Gay Identity

*Pre-publication
REVIEWS,
COMMENTARIES,
EVALUATIONS . . .*

"**O**utrageous and warm, serious and laugh-out-loud funny—*The Mentor* is all these things and more, a fiercely original book that's like nothing I've ever read. In its tender investigation of a friendship, and in its willingness to take on received notions of family, church, and identity, Jay Quinn's book challenges us—regardless of who we are—to be more fully human."

Paul Lisicky
Author of *Lawnboy*,
Provincetown, MA

"**J**ay Quinn has woven together the tangled contradictions of what it means to be both gay and Southern into a tapestry that is equal parts spiritual and sensual. *The Mentor* is an exploration of Quinn's love/hate relationship with the South and his metamorphosis from drugged-out surfer to thoughtful adult. Guiding him is his wise mentor, Joe, who shows Quinn the way by living it. *The Mentor* describes Jay's journey through the bars of Norfolk and the beaches of Hatteras. This memoir is a window on a world of hot sex and broken hearts, flirtation and lasting friendship, frivolity and the search for meaning."

Elizabeth Brownrigg
Author of *Falling to Earth*,
Durham, NC

More pre-publication
REVIEWS, COMMENTARIES, EVALUATIONS . . .

"**J**ay Quinn's exploration of the mentoring process within the gay community—of being taken under a wing, of being taught by the more mature, of learning from someone trusted—shines with honest grace. He has taken the very personal and amplified it into an exemplar for a community that has a lengthy, noble tradition of the older guiding the younger; but it is a tradition not much honored in our writing or in our public lives. This memoir, candid and humane, intimate and witty, is an eloquent recognition of what one generation can teach another."

Richard Labonte
General Manager,
A Different Light Bookstores,
San Francisco, CA

"**W**hen you read Jay Quinn's *The Mentor*, it's as if you're reading a book written by two different men, complementary and sympatico. One is a Southern storyteller, the kind that has made the South famous for its rich literary history—you can hear Quinn spinning a yarn up on the front porch, offering any number of juicy, scandalous stories, confiding a couple of secrets, keeping a couple more to himself. And there's another writer, a thoughtful scholar who knows how to tell a tale on the page as well as the porch, who can look at his own life with enough wisdom to convey to others what he has learned. And that is what *The Mentor* is all about—teaching and telling each other effortlessly, the reader and writer at once protégé and professor."

Brian Bouldrey
Writer and Editor,
San Francisco, CA

"**I**n this alternately funny and moving memoir, Jay Quinn spins a tale that is both intensely personal and touchingly familiar. The story of his ongoing friendship with the man who helped him discover his place in the gay world is a story about the intense connections that form the basis of so many lifelong gay friendships. Reading it, we are reminded of the unique beauty of the families we choose for ourselves, and reminded, too, that whoever we are we have something to share with the world."

Michael Thomas Ford
Lambda Literary Award-Winning
Author of *Alec Baldwin*
Doesn't Love Me
and *That's Mr. Faggot to You,*
Jamaica Plain, MA

The Mentor
A Memoir of Friendship and Gay Identity

HAWORTH Gay & Lesbian Studies
John P. De Cecco, PhD
Editor in Chief

The Mentor
A Memoir of Friendship and Gay Identity

Jay Quinn

Harrington Park Press®
An Imprint of The Haworth Press, Inc.
New York • London • Oxford

Published by

Harrington Park Press®, an imprint of The Haworth Press, Inc., 10 Alice Street, Binghamton, NY
13904-1580

Cover design by Jennifer M. Gaska.

The Library of Congress has cataloged the hardcover edition of this book as:

Quinn, Jay.
   The mentor : a memoir of friendship and gay identity / Jay Quinn.
      p.cm.
   ISBN 0-7890-0496-8 (hc : alk. paper)
   1. Quinn, Jay. 2. Riddick, Joe. 3. Gay men—United States—Biography. 4. Mentoring—United
States—Case studies. 5. Gays—United States—Identity—Case studies. I. Title.

HQ75.8.A-Z.Q56 A3 2000
305.38'9664'0973—dc21   99-056495

ISBN: 1-56023-937-9 (pbk.)

. . . Just give me many chances
I'll see you through it all
just give me time to learn to crawl . . .

from "Stewart's Coat"
Ricki Lee Jones

ABOUT THE AUTHOR

Jay Quinn is a native of coastal North Carolina. He currently works as a copywriter and a book reviewer. Mr. Quinn graduated from East Carolina University in 1979. He has held many occupations, such as art director, illustrator, video director, and independent writer, director, and producer. He now lives in South Florida with his partner of seven years and their two huge Doberman/Labrador Retriever mixed-breed dogs.

CONTENTS

Author's Note

Where necessary or requested, I have changed the names of some of the participants in my past. History may be a consensus, but memoir is clearly from a single skewed perspective. Memories come with names and feelings and presents that may be vastly different from the pasts shared intensely and left behind in the unrelenting pull of diverging wants, needs, and destinies.

Although the following ideas are my own, I do not solely own my past. So, I acknowledge now any difference in viewpoint of anyone who may be intimately or tangentially described in the work that follows. Remember, memory has a way of coloring some things in bright, broad strokes while fading others to ghosts. In that same way, time and tide really do change everything as we accrete and erode against one another along the way.

Foreword

We are holden to men by every sort of tie, by blood, by pride, by fear, by hope, by lucre, by lust, by hate, by admiration, by every circumstance and badge and trifle—but we can scarce believe that so much character can subsist in another as to draw us by love.

"Friendship"
Ralph Waldo Emerson

Nearly hidden amid the lush and gaudy overgrowth of mainstream heterosexual America is a trail of homosexual mentors—gay adults whose steps and experience guide the staggering efforts of gay youth—that leads back as far as ancient Greece and forward as far as our hopeful imaginations can take us. As an artist, a writer, a lover, and a man, Jay Quinn has followed that path, and *The Mentor* is the literary and celebratory record of his journey.

Although you wouldn't know it by the popular demonization of the modern gay lifestyle—an apparent emotional junkyard littered with reckless pickups and burned-out hedonists—there has long been a tradition of fatherly one-on-one, man-to-man mentoring that continues to be gently upheld around the world. And just as the twenty-four-year-old Truman Capote was chaperoned around Paris by Jean Cocteau (affectionately calling his charge "the infant"), and a teenage James Baldwin was befriended, nurtured, and lovingly raised in Greenwich Village by the flamboyant painter Beauford Delaney, in a later decade and a very different part of the world, another writer-to-be was led forward by the hand of an elder man. Jay Quinn's now seventeen-year allegiance with Joe Riddick began

Nicholas Weinstock, a writer and teacher in New York City, is the author of *The Secret Love of Sons.* His articles and essays have been featured on National Public Radio and in *New York Times Magazine, The Nation, Vogue, Glamour, Elle, US,* and many other publications.

when Quinn was twenty-three and his newly begun life was "just ending its continental shift into a full acceptance of a gay identity." From that day, Quinn directs us generously onward—as he was directed generously onward—through his initiations, both sensual and emotional, through his rowdy social trials and silent personal wrestlings, and through his hesitant and often bumbling attempts to "climb up Joe's backbone" to a place of comfort, wisdom, and love.

If the voyage is rarely a happy romp, and hardly a straightforward march (as there is no "gay" learning process, as the author advises us early on, "no queer werewolf whose single violent caress makes you long to hang drapes"), we could not ask for a better guide and narrator than Jay Quinn. With welcome humor, thorough insight, and a fierce candor that dares to throw light on everything from the intolerance of churches to the struggles of fidelity to the callous sexual antics of his own twenty-something self, he shows gayness to be a human and humane identity, while showing respect for the man who helped him to achieve it. His homosexuality, he explains, is every bit as awkward and inevitable as his left-handedness, every bit as urgent as life itself. And while homage is movingly paid to the various influences of family, friends, teachers, and idols, only someone who's gone through the same trials by fire can lead a younger man coolly through the leaps and dances that await him.

"Ultimately, and precisely in the deepest and most important matters, we are unspeakably alone," wrote Rainer Maria Rilke to the apprentice famous for corresponding with him in *Letters to a Young Poet,* "and many things must happen, many things must go right, a whole constellation of events must be fulfilled, for one human being to successfully advise or help another." Indeed, many things happen to gay men as they emerge into the straight and narrow world—some of them right, many of them wrong—but it was when Joe Riddick happened to Jay Quinn that a sky full of glimmering possibilities opened before him like a map. One can only wish that we were all lucky enough to be gifted with such an earthly miracle of friendship. We are lucky enough to have the brave book that that friendship produced.

Nicholas Weinstock
New York City

Acknowledgments

This book certainly wouldn't have come about without the care of the following people. My good friend, first editor, and de facto agent, Nicholas Weinstock. My "family of blood": Mom and Dad, Glenn, and Brenda. My "out-laws": Mark and Steve; Rick, Anita, and Alex; Gene and Maggie. My "family of choice": Brad Moyer, Joe Barnes, Susan Highsmith, C. C. Kaplan, and Mary Beth McAuley. The Singer Island crew. For inspiration and encouragement, Jill McCorkle. For the soundtrack, Ricki Lee Jones. At The Haworth Press: Melissa Devendorf, Steve Zeeland, and Bill Palmer.

And of course, Joe Riddick, who is everything except my heart, Jeff Auchter.

Introduction

Mentoring and Gay Identity

Erastes and *Eromenos,* the Lover and Beloved. In the highly romanticized and eroticized mythology of the gay world, the notion of the older man taking the trusting younger one under his wing and into his arms to provide tutelage in the experience of maleness is one of wistful longing. In the suspicious and demonizing mythology of contemporary Christian cults, that same notion has been the seedbed of a pervasive idea of inherent pedophilia in all gay experience. Oddly, both perceptions are perversions of the original concept of mentoring and male bonding as practiced by the ancient Greeks.

Among the Cretan, the Lakedaemonian, and Attic societies of pre-Christian times, a ritualized form of homosexual courtship and bonding among men and youths did exist. Such relationships served a variety of purposes in essentially militaristic, phallocentric, male-oriented societies. They were seen to be a reinforcing part of a society that valued women only as soulless, morally corrupting brood stock, while the status of maleness was considered more than halfway to the attainment of perfection of body and soul. Such were the times.

What seems to have been lost in the nostalgic longing of the gay community for an archaic male-celebrating society and the hysterical cant of the religious right is the idea of honor in the relationship between the *erastes* and the *eromenos.* Such relationships strived to embody honor and a certain moral rightness. In the gymnasiums and agoras of Periclean Athens, simply sexual arrangements were considered as sleazy and base as any contemporary party circuit *khouros kalon,* tricking for status with an older man. A slut is a slut, in ancient Attica or in contemporary South Beach.

1

What gay youth does not wish for someone older and wiser to appear and say, "This is your path. This is the way"? I will admit to being seduced by any number of Mary Renault novels. How much easier it would have been to walk that early way behind a tall Achilles to my following Patroklos. Of course, I am the product of a particularly pragmatic Southern Baptist background. I doubt I would have willingly traded a piece of my ass for an uncertain promise of being led into the full light of manhood. No, honor would have definitely had to play a part in the deal. I don't particularly equate the notion of honor with romantic antiquity.

Honor has everything to do with respect. I am fortunate to have parents who respect my physical person, my inherent, if unformed intelligence, and my spirit. That has been my experience. My experience informed me that love is bound together with honoring another person. Honoring another person involves taking the whole person into account when forming the construct of the relationship. From that basic grounding, I developed my stance in looking for others who would honor me in return.

Ancient wine cups with etched black and red figures often bear the inscription of a name followed by the phrase "is beautiful." Such wine cups frequently were love offerings from an *erastes* to an *eromenos*. One doesn't see a name inscribed followed by the phrase "has a hot ass" or "a fat cock." The intent of the cup was to say that all of the beloved was beautiful—face, body, and soul. No particular body part, from a square chest to a lively intellect, was singled out for appreciation. No. Honor was given to the whole being of the beloved. Any reduction of the admired youth to a mere fuck toy would have been a mortal insult.

How can one become a mentor or be mentored without some concept of honor or respect? Many gay people are brutalized as youths. The number of adolescent suicides is higher among gay youngsters. Queer bashing remains a blood sport, in Texas, Wyoming, Alabama, and even in Manhattan, Miami, and San Francisco. There is also that physical and emotional damage which older gay men casually inflict on gay children in their headlong rush to explore and embrace sexual experience.

I was no exception to brutality against my physical self or my psyche by an essentially straight world. Without disrespecting those who remain wounded far more than I, I maintain that victimhood is self-perpetuating in some ways. An erosion of the fundamental sense of self occurs when one lives in an atmosphere of incessant, subtle and overt criticism, surveillance, and condemnation. No less demeaning is the cannibalization of one's innocence by other gay men. Collectively, these emotional onslaughts create a septic environment of psychological victimhood.

Ultimately, one can devalue oneself to the point where no respect is asked in anticipation of its denial. All of us have found bad mentors on the path to becoming gay adults. The fact remains, however, that the quest for that mentor, that strong and wise *erastes* to our own innocent *eromenos,* is an essential part of our maturation.

For good or ill, we come with a set of parents and family histories that serve to provide a foundation for our sense of self and our world. Development of moral and spiritual stances, socialization skills, as well as physical and mental nurture are the province of our blood families for the early parts of our lives. With the growing assertion of a gay identity, these traditional forms of instruction and nurture lose relevance to a burgeoning sense of a whole other world in which we are compelled to dwell.

At some point, the schizoid disjunct between our blood families' social constructs and our own drives us into alien territory. Who then comes to instruct and nurture? There can be younger lovers, there can be those our own age, but in a sense, each is a case of the blind leading the blind. By instinct and conditioning, we look to those older than ourselves to provide examples and to socialize us into the larger community.

As the oldest sibling in my family, and as a perpetually arrogant and self-absorbed teenager, I recall being pestered by my baby brother to tell him everything about entering high school. It seemed his questions were endless and needlessly naive. I finally demanded to know why he was worrying the hell out of me with something so simple. In an equally exasperated innocence, he replied that I had been where he had to go.

It is really very simple. This is how we learn and how we grow. If for the duration of this discussion of mentoring and gay identity we can suspend either our impulse to a romantic ideal or a gut-level

aversion to an exaggerated notion of experience debauching innocence, perhaps we can see the fullness of treating one another as
complete people, not as body parts in eroticized combinations or
free-floating perversions. Although the experience of mentoring
may have a sexual component, this is not its raison d'être.

For the purposes of this discussion, I should like to hold forth a
concept of mentoring as a fully involved emotional relationship, not
especially a sexual one. For this discussion and its illustration, my
own relationship with my most important mentor, the concept of
mentoring and the development of a gay identity revolves around
honor.

In this sense, honor has everything to do with respect for each
participant in the relationship. For me, respect is the critical component of honor—honor being that sense of taking into account, and
respecting, the mentored as a whole being, not a cafeteria assort-
ment of highly prized parts.

Being simply human first, and only then a member of a subset
identified as "gay," how we develop as gay people is fundamentally
not different in any way from how we grow from infancy to adolescence to adulthood. We learn from direct experience and by example. We receive positive and negative reinforcement from the application of our acquisition of information, and then we assimilate
those stimuli into our functioning process. There is no specifically
gay learning process. Though we purportedly have smaller hypo-
thalamuses than our heterosexually oriented brothers, the process
by which we accumulate wisdom has never been deemed fundamentally different.

Likewise, mentoring is related to gay identity only within an
artificially constructed gay context. This discussion is only relevant
if one recognizes the dissonance between being reared in a heterosexual construct and finding oneself, inexplicably, in an altogether
different one as an adult. In an era that celebrates differences (or
not) almost to the point of hysteria, I find it tiresome, if necessary to
say, in this instance, that gay identity is different, but only because
the artificiality of the construction of a gay context is something
imposed by a predominately heterosexual world.

That said, mentoring is fundamental to survival when one finds
oneself living in the equivalent of a carnival mirror fun house. It is

absolutely necessary to be taught what is genuine in such a highly artificial existence. When all of one's most genuine feelings, such as desire, love, and the quest for human connection, are seen as mere reflections of the true or correct image and thus suspect, at best, or hated, at worst, personal perception is everything.

Mirror images are hard realities to walk into when our learned perceptions are not to be trusted. In the development of a gay identity, the mentor serves as the subtle translator between the perceived reality and the real one. Oral tradition, stories, and humor serve as teaching aids to help us discern the limits of an outwardly imposed artificiality and the genuine in a functioning gay identity. How else do we define who we are in this alien, yet familiar, world?

Last year, my straight suburban neighborhood underwent a sea change. My next-door neighbor kicked out her husband and moved in her boy's Little League coach. My neighbor across the street walked out on her husband of fifteen years, leaving him to rear their two daughters. My partner and I were the most stable couple on the block. We have become a mirror image of suburban normality, without police responses to domestic disputes or restraining orders. Our house is indiscernible from the others, without even a hint of hysterical landscaping, just a few typical leggy hibiscus shrubs and a coconut palm in need of a trim.

A friend of mine, a circuit queen, needlessly defending his life, once told me that gay people spent so many years in the closet as young people that fantasy became more comforting than reality. For this clearly defined gay subculture, one of the by-products of so much hard-won liberation was to bring the fantasy world born in the closet out with them. Thus, Ecstasy, Special K, and hypnotic artificial electronic music are sacramental in the communally celebrated liberation from the erotic desolation of the closet.

Suburban assimilation to hyper-queer. So we live, the extremes of the post-Stonewall generation, the generation of AIDS. Who would not need a guide entering that fun house existence in 1981? Without someone to make sense of it, I might still be there. Coming out in the early 1980s, I missed the orgy but still caught the lingering scent of spilled poppers and the stench of black leather before they were overtaken by the colder, deadlier odors of hospital corridors and latex. I'm glad my identity had a mentor. I had no idea what I was getting myself into.

I met Joe Riddick when I was twenty-three years old. Even at that age, I was still a child in many ways. My life was just ending its continental shift into a full acceptance of a gay identity. Like a parent, but in a way no blood parent could, Joe undertook the nurturing of that identity. That nurture was something I rather selfishly took for granted, until I began work on this book.

I asked Joe, rather baldly, what made him take on raising me. With the selfsame laugh that I first heard the day I met him, untarnished by seventeen years of wear and tear, he told me it was all part of the tradition. "Do you remember me telling you stories about Bill Poole?" Joe asked. "Mother Poole?" I responded, recalling literally dozens of stories about that feisty and doomed queen who figured so large in the narrative of Joe's coming out.

Joe looked at me with knowing tenderness that I have rarely seen outside my mother's or father's face. "Son, when you came out, it was easy. It was a lot different for us before you. It's almost an obligation for us old queers to take you young'uns under our wing. I did it for you because Bill Poole did it for me. I always looked at it like it was my duty."

I spent most of the twenty-three years before meeting Joe Riddick in a world I perceived to be, if not deliberately hostile, then snickeringly disdainful of a very real part of myself. Life sharpens its claws in a variety of ways on everyone. I cannot claim victimhood in enduring those assaults common to all humanity, but there is a comforting balm of commonality in heterosexual experience that is withheld for an extended period of time from homosexuals. Finding that balm and the joy in its comfort is what this story is all about. I, too, must honor the tradition.

In line at the bank one morning not too long ago, I stood behind two boys, a blond maybe sixteen years old and a dark-haired studlet who looked to be no more than a year older. They were far too intimate in proximity and betrayed by their solicitousness toward each other. The dark one spoke low toward the blond one's ear, and I watched the blush creep up under the faint, blond down on his neck to redden his impossibly fresh face.

I had to force back my panic. I wanted to protect them from themselves, the openness of their affection. I wanted to say, "You boys better cool it, or somebody's gonna catch you in the parking lot and beat the shit out of you." I searched the bored, preoccupied faces of the others in line. No one cared; no one else saw or chose to see. No one else but me even noticed. The line advanced, and the two boys proceeded to the next teller, together. The dark one's hand was pressed in the small of the other's back, gently steering him.

My deposit made, I found my way to my truck, passing them in the parking lot where they stood by their car. The dark one lit a cigarette and offered it to the other. I caught a snatch of their discussion of which movie they were going to see. All around them, the commerce of the day passed, oblivious. No one spat "faggot" at them. After twenty years, there is some reward in the visibility, meager equity earned by a plague. At least in some places, being out is not really an issue if you've never been in. However, that ease in equality is in no way universal.

I started my truck and envied those two kids a little—partly for being so young, partly for their ability to see each other so clearly in the fog of their own raging hormones. I also envied them their freedom from the poisonous self-policing that I had done so diligently at that age. I envied them the beloved uncle who was gay, and it was no big deal, as I, myself, am a gay uncle, and it's no big deal.

Inside, I knew that first love is never perfect, no matter how tolerant the environment. I wondered to whom they would turn when they moved from the warm circle of their parents' ability or willingness to counsel them on a broken heart, or a faithless partner. I wondered who would get them in at the Copa, or lend them books by Mary Renault and Gordon Merrick. Who would teach them not to take Percodan on an empty stomach, or what to do if they got crabs? Who would they call first when they got their results from an anonymous HIV test? I wondered who would tell them, as Joe Riddick had told me and Bill Poole had told him, about the old days, from *erastes* and *eromenos* to The Pet Shop Boys.

I wondered . . . and I came home to work on this book.

Chapter 1

A Short Queer History

March is a cruel month on the northeastern coast of North Carolina, not for the sudden nor'easters, nor for the desolation of a summer resort's bright tackiness humbled by winter's cold light. No, March is cruel for containing the aching promise of sunshine and opportunity on the horizon, but not yet arrived.

Growing up gay, that is essentially the landscape I inhabited, internally and externally. March 1982 was like all the Marches of all the years that preceded it. But that one March changed my life. I found a friend, an older brother, a father, and a teacher—all in the lanky form of Joe Riddick. Seventeen years later, it is no overstatement to say Joe is the reason I survived as a gay man.

At twenty-three, the Outer Banks was the only place I had ever found empty enough to contain the growing emptiness in me. I knew I was gay, but I wasn't quite sure what that had to do with anything, outside of a dark car or a bedroom redolent with the scent of beer, bong hits, and furtiveness. Needless to say, I was miserable. I was getting "it" on a regular basis from a surfing buddy of mine, but I was well grounded in the code that "it" didn't have anything to do with me, or at least those parts of me that were inconvenient, like my heart or mind.

When you live long enough denying that you have a heart and a mind, a sort of psychic wind begins to whistle around that void inside you with the force of a hurricane. Similar to most gay youngsters growing up before the current climate of emphasis on self-esteem, my identity as a gay person was all internal; my self-esteem was based on my ability to maintain my defensive coloration.

On the outside, I was a typical surfer with a low-skill job and a taste for buds—the beer and the bong kind, but not the boy kind.

That taste was as well hidden as my preference for soul divas and the talent to create words and pictures that showed my true colors.

As for gay role models, they were distant, if not nonexistent. Whispers and rumors, raised eyebrows and tightened mouths were my indicators from family and peers that any individual likely to be gay was one to be avoided strenuously. Despite the widening void of my own emptiness, my outside image had to be maintained at all costs, for self-esteem, if not literal survival. That was my rationalization anyway. Rationalization has an odd way of becoming truth.

Then, too, I had my own prejudice against the effeminate men who were most visible as potential role models. Truth be told, my fantasies, inclinations, and identity ran more to men who could shingle a roof than to those who could play a hymn with such haunting feeling that an entire congregation of Southern Baptists would rush to redemption. I liked to build stuff. I liked to smell new wood and ride around in trucks. I didn't want to grow lovely roses and play contract bridge.

In my youth, arrogance, and isolation, I thought that particular identity was the only alternative. Resolute and obstinate in my shabby butch posturing, I decided that it was better to have all of nothing than to settle for less than I wanted. I was a rawboned blond mountain, waiting obstinately for the arrival of my gay Mohammed.

Does this sound like self-loathing? Maybe it does, but it has taken me seventeen years to acquire a starter set of Wedgwood china, much longer to understand that I have sensibilities that go beyond the blue-collar closet that I spent so much time constructing. I can tell you when the understanding began.

In that cold March of 1982, I worked for a land surveying and engineering firm in Nags Head. The office was located on the third floor of a building that housed a construction-cum-realty firm. I had struck up a friendship with one of the sales staff. Suzanne was lithe, fey, and wild as a bat. With unerring instinct, she learned, first, that I was an artist, as was she, and, second, that I was doing more than surfing with a certain general construction worker.

Suzanne scared the shit out of me, but I had reached such a level of weariness with my own lies, isolation, and duplicity that, I imagine, she was taken aback by the storm of honesty she encountered when a small dope deal earned her my confidence. She said, "You have to meet my friend Joe."

Suzanne said Joe was wonderful, talented, and fun. When they had been roommates in the tiny collection of apartments in Kitty Hawk known as Lovely Shelby Village, they had cut an omnivorous sexual swath through all the opportunities available to them on the Outer Banks. Suzanne liked to compare herself and Joe to Mona Ramsey and Michael "Mouse" in Armistead Maupin's *Tales of the City*. It was a glamorous, sophisticated, and apt comparison.

I was aware that I wanted, and needed, more glamour and sophistication in my life. My social life consisted mainly of hanging out with my surfer buddies, listening to the Allman Brothers, and getting high. I wanted to talk about things. I wanted to go places. Hell, I wanted to dance. Suzanne's description of her friendship with Joe was like the promise of spring.

Still, from Suzanne's description of Joe and what he did for a living, I decided that politeness was in order, but the last person I wanted to meet and hang out with was the only interior designer in a county that numbered only five thousand year-round residents. Why not just have "I'm a big queer" tattooed on my face instead?

I managed to put off any contact with Joe until one day, after work, I sauntered downstairs to Suzanne's office to drop off a nickel bag of pot. Seated across from her at her desk was a man, dressed in a business suit and wearing very trendy and very cool red-framed schoolboy glasses. I was aware I was being assessed, but I chalked it up more to being out of place, dressed as I was for a day's work outside. With my fingers holding a bag of pot inside my jeans pocket, I tried to cover my discomfort and true reason for my presence by asking Suzanne if she knew where I could buy some plantains.

The man stretched his six-foot-four frame in his chair as lithely as a jungle cat. In a deep voice, he asked me why in the world I wanted plantains. There was no insinuation in his question, but a warning bell vibrated deep in my defensive core. I was suddenly aware that plantains were first cousins to bananas and bananas were first cousins to penises. I remember saying awkwardly that I was tired of winter and I guessed I was in sort of a Coco-Caribe state of mind. The elegant man looked at me incredulously and then began to laugh. His laughter was warm and inclusive, despite the sheer ludicrousness of my response.

Suzanne said, "Jay, this is my friend Joe." I smiled. Joe unfolded from his seat and stood, offering his hand for shaking. I offered my own paw and was pleased to find it engulfed in a handshake as firm, dry, and welcoming as I'd ever known. "Well, son," Joe drawled, his height and self-assurance exaggerating the six-year difference in our ages, "I don't know where you can get plantains, but if you think they'd get rid of these winter blues, I think I'd fly to Cuba to get some."

I recall little more of that first meeting than my unnerving gaffe and Joe's easy response. I do recall a sense of immediate comfort and acceptance that I had never experienced on meeting a stranger. Whatever else was said, that first meeting ended with a tentative dinner invitation extended from Joe to Suzanne and me. After a lifetime of reserve, I can only now appreciate the degree of security or long-suppressed need I must have felt to accept.

Sometimes spring comes with an abruptness that almost makes one wish for the shelter of winter. The sun is suddenly bright, the air is warm, the absence of cold is missed as much as the familiar weight of a heavy coat. So spring came to the Outer Banks of North Carolina in late March 1982. In that same turning of seasons, I began to grow.

I needed, at twenty-three, to be led toward some semblance of self-acceptance. I needed to come out. Unwittingly, over a clumsy exchange of pleasantries about plantains, in a near-deserted, queer-bashing corner of the world, I met Joe Riddick, who could show me the way. Mohammed had come to the mountain. I had found my mentor.

Not too long after that night, Suzanne and I went to dinner at Joe's apartment. Recalling it now, I feel an easy longing for that place and that time. People's homes often say more about them in an instant than months of casual acquaintance can reveal. Joe's place did.

On the second floor of a quadruplex just outside the entrance to Nags Head Woods, Joe's apartment felt immediately like home. I lived in a prefabricated house on stilts perched in the scrubby dunes of Avalon Beach. Although the place was mine, and I loved it with all the tenacity and daydreams one does one's first house, my tenancy seemed tenuous. Joe's place seemed certain.

Every wall in the house was covered in art of various degrees of fame or fond familiarity. The arrangement was highly idiosyncratic. A movie poster for the film *Making Love* hung cheek by jowl with a photo print of Walker Evans and a sincere (if really bad) watercolor by an old friend. The effect was almost overwhelming. Each piece promised a story. It was a promise that fulfilled itself over the years.

The large apartment's single wall not covered in art was crammed with sagging shelves of books. It was a treasure trove of titles that spilled from the shelves to become stacks on the floor. I scanned the titles with all the hunger and absorption of a kid in a candy store. My literacy and book hunger had been seriously deprived since I moved to the beach. My current boyfriend and buddies fell asleep reading album cover liner notes.

For all the treasure in the spare bedroom/library, the kitchen held far more. The kitchen was the heart of Joe's home. Joe ushered Suzanne and me to the table in the box-bay window of the kitchen's south end. Suzanne took her place at the table's side, and I slid into a cut-down pew that Joe off-handedly remarked was from some desanctified church near Charleston.

Worn smooth by the asses of the faithful and fitted with generous cushions, the old pew held me like a comforting hand. Joe served us both with a drink and an ashtray before moving to the stove in the kitchen's north end. As he and Suzanne talked, he conjured up a feast of fried chicken, butter beans, sliced tomatoes, rice, and biscuits.

Silent, I listened to the rich conversation and enjoyed the richer aromas of cooking. The animated conversation between Joe and Suzanne kept their attention, allowing me to minutely examine the rest of the kitchen from my vantage point. On the countertop by the sink was a lamp made from a ceramic figurine of a Mandarin fisherman, posed forever trudging home with a basket on his back. On the wall next to it hung a print of gray brushwork cypress trees on a tender celadon-colored field, framed in old mahogany molding.

This odd little tableau stuck in my mind with disarming sweetness. As the room dimmed during dinner's completion and consumption, the lamp's glow and the serenity of the print merged into a still life of comfort to me. Homely domesticity is holy in its own way, and the traditions of hospitality are older than Christianity. Finding these elements in a stranger's home allowed a certain sense of familiarity to disarm me. As unlike my grandmother's kitchen as any could be, I felt a growing sense of safety there that was as familiar—that same sense of coming home.

In the following summer months, I came to eat at that table more often than I did at my own. It became Joe's habit to call me as I was getting off work to say, "What you want for dinner, baby? I'm in a mood to mix some groceries." I'd find my way back to my spot on the pew again after a quick surf session or shower to get rid of the sweat and grime from working outside. I'd watch Joe cook and sing along with the radio, tuned to WOWI, a soul station out of Norfolk. Any song could summon a memory for him. From the memory, he could spin a story.

It was during those long summer suppers, perched with the setting sun on my back, that I began to learn from Joe's stories of the greater gay world. I learned of tea dances and queer cotillions, of drag queens and horny marines. I learned of dirty bookstores and discos, of romance and redemption, of sex and broken-glass break-ups. In the midst of it all strode Joe as the central character.

With laughter, Joe pushed away the seaminess, with snapping fingers, the disappointments and slurs. With seriousness, he recounted the happiness, and with insouciance, the joy. Surprisingly, his narrative of childhood was as familiar as my own backyard. It was as if he attended the same Southern Baptist church, the same school, or lived down the same street as I did growing up. But Joe's narrative continued along streets and spots and places I had never allowed myself to go.

I always went home after these suppers with a cache of books under my arm that Joe thought I had to read. Joe introduced me to Holleran, Picano, White, and Merrick. He also introduced me to my own hunger for some stories of my own, unaware that I was to become a part of Joe's story and he of mine.

I could not deny or discount the mounting impatience I felt with myself. I came to believe that my retarded growth as a queer had more to do with cowardice than anything else. I hadn't really changed socially since high school. My straight boyfriend and all my friends were still getting stoned and watching reruns of *The Twilight Zone.* The growing disjunct between who I was and who I presented myself to be was creating my own Twilight Zone.

Joe's stories, so familiar and unalien, were awakening me to the awareness that sex and love were all around me. Real life was all around me. After years of putting so much effort into creating an entire separate identity for myself, I had used up much energy and honesty that could have been better spent. I became increasingly aware, by comparison and contrast with Joe's experience, that I was not living an authentic life. Joe saw that. In a way, he rescued me.

My own self-absorption was such that I never considered for very long why Joe had taken such a deep and sudden interest in my education as a queer. I had such a sense of fastidiousness about myself that I never considered being soiled by anyone else's needs. I was a selfish little fucker in some ways, and in many others, I was still naive as hell. For the most part, I was simply playing my long-standing role as the eldest child.

If I saw myself as something precious and new, a thing to be celebrated and tended, it was by no dearth of experience in that regard. I simply assumed Joe had come along to take my education in hand. It was my due. After all, I was totally guileless in becoming his friend.

God, I was such a child. At twenty-three, I really didn't grasp the fundamentals of queer economics on its most basic level. Innocence, a tight body, and a knowing grin are capital that diminishes with every passing year. I wanted to believe that Joe was happy watching me spend my share. I was unwilling to think he might want an investment in himself in return.

At twenty-three, I looked eighteen. What had been a curse in the junior high locker room became a blessing on the beach in 1982. I had always been a pretty boy, but that summer saw the firming of my jawline and the maturation of my looks as a man. I had always resented the lag time in my physical transition from mere prettiness to something more on the lines of masculine appeal.

As a result, I tended to discount what I looked like, beyond an honest vanity based on hygiene rather than pride. I always held myself up to Jan Michael Vincent's mirror and came away rather disappointed. Looking back now, I see that I was appealing physically, but I remain convinced that I was more appealing intellectually. Initially, Joe entertained some thoughts of the physical, but in a flash of self-preservation, he decided I was a far better prospect as a neophyte than as a lover.

As with much else, Joe's perception of the situation was really apt. We have been friends and family now for almost twenty years. If we'd been lovers, we would have cut each other's throats long ago. What has endured and grown is something that is unique in my life. I can count fewer than five friendships that have endured as long or longer.

For Joe's friendship, I am all the richer. Hopefully, so is he. Together and separately, we experienced an extraordinary time in history, generally, and gay history, specifically. In our lifetimes, great social change occurred. Freedoms were bitterly bought and bitterly challenged. A firestorm of disease swept through our landscape, and, humbly, we still stand.

Children of an age, Joe and I walked its terrain on our own terms. We forged a great history, not in New York or San Francisco, but in Tidewater Virginia and coastal North Carolina. History is most often experienced intimately in small places and in small lives. Hopefully, this short course on queer history will reveal what it meant to grow and love and live as my mentor and I did.

Chapter 2

The Common World

Thumbing back in my mental journal through late adolescence to childhood, the pages are written in small type that tediously reveals a long march to self-autonomy. For the most part, I believe my life began only when I moved to the beach at the age of twenty-two. On my own terms, I took a job. I packed my stuff, strapped my surfboard to the racks on the roof of my car, and headed to the literal edge of the earth.

I rented a six-hundred-square-foot house on stilts in the Avalon Beach section of Kill Devil Hills and set about building my life. Everything that had gone before was based on a series of expectations imposed on me from external sources. Those expectations made anything of my own doing feel amateurish, like stumbling toward the light.

Name one person who claims to have enjoyed a totally carefree, prosaic childhood and I'll show you a politician or marketing executive. The reality of childhood and adolescence is never as sanitized or innocent as the images ad men create or politicians presume to defend. Of course, reality won't sell toilet bowl cleaner or tract houses. Politicians building a platform on family values won't be elected by voters who are busily breeding little consumers if they treat the messy, frustrating experience of childhood in anything other than idealized terms.

I don't idealize my childhood, despite the efforts of an extraordinary set of parents and my beloved grandmother, each of whom took much delight in the process of my becoming a fully realized grown-up, while I variously hated and enjoyed it. My mother would tell you I was "born grown."

Perhaps for that reason, I can't go back to childhood for very long. I can't breathe in that restricted space. Neither can Joe, for his own reasons. In the conversations that formed the basis of this book, childhood was revisited only as often and as dutifully as one might visit an oral surgeon. The subsequent mining of those times was only necessary to prove a point, one that bore fruit in an adult context.

Why is this return to the vivid Technicolor world of childhood such a chore? Both Joe and I come from homes unscarred by divorce, hunger, or abuse. To any casual observer, it appeared that our parents spared no effort to ensure our health, our education, or our well-being. That is the truth. Knowing we were loved personally and not in the abstract doesn't explain memory's subtle bleaching of the colors of childhood into the dim black and white of recall.

For gay children, regardless of birth order, growing up as unique, if beloved, entities within a heterosexual context is an isolating experience. From the beginning, we are isolated from our families in some ways. We are simultaneously alien and familiar to parents and siblings alike. Although sexual identity is, in many ways, as predetermined as eye color or race, its exercise, acceptance, and expression are delayed by a host of other factors. Inarguably, the primary factor is the family.

In the 1950s, and arguably even today, there was no consensus on how gay people come to be. Most generally, we appear singly in a family that, by its very construction, is alien to who we are and what we will become. Yet, that family forms us and provides the foundation on which we will try to construct the meaningful relationships of our lives. Unfortunately, a great deal of that foundation is built on deception.

For gay children, the lies we tell ourselves and those around us undergo a rapid maturation. Dishonesty serves to protect us and those we love from every reaction to our fear of abandonment, from presumed disappointment to outright anger. Protective colorization is a means of survival no less for the queer kid than for the brown wren or common chameleon. Thus, the internal closet is born, and with it a whole context for dealing with the world.

By natural extension, the social environment gay people are born into is not built to accommodate us. Still, though alternately hostile and benign, that social environment provides gay people with the same layers of secondary identity that it gives to the larger heterosexual hegemony. Every individual has a social identity, a cultural identity, a frame of reference from which to relate to the world.

The homosexual context of relating to the world, although internalized, is as demanding in practice as left-handedness. All those who believe homosexuality is a choice, or some willful embrace of "aberrant" behavior, are self-deluded, if not purposefully ignorant. Being both homosexual and left-handed, I have related to the larger world from those frames of reference for as long as I can remember.

The only willful embrace the queer kid rushes to is the safe embrace of the closet, but that cruelly narrows the kid's outward view. It is amazing how many gay people actively disavow, distance themselves from, or reconceptualize their identities after adolescence. A closet cannot accommodate the rich past or heritage into which the gay child is born. That heritage is one from which the child presumes to be excluded by his or her very existence. Arriving as the newest addition to a long line of ancestors who settled into each phase of life with daunting conformity, the queer kid has to question his or her relevance in the history of the family, neighborhood, town, and even era.

To paraphrase Joseph Campbell by substituting "queer" for "hero," there is a great deal of validity, even satisfaction, in a life spent trudging the familiar paths around the village compound. Historically speaking, however, the nascent queer must follow bliss outside those familiar paths to seek his or her destiny.

That has been the cultural imperative for gay people, an astounding population forced to migrate in some way to actualize the need for community, for context, and for love. Witness Manhattan, Miami, Atlanta, and San Francisco, to name a few gay ideations of Mecca. To reiterate the point is to wallow in cliché.

I myself have become a cliché. After many years of slow emotional starvation in North Carolina, I moved to South Florida in 1991. I was as much a refugee as if I had arrived on a raft across heavy seas, instead of in a 1982 Toyota station wagon in heavy traffic on I-95. There are many ways to escape oppression.

Here, I have found much happiness. Here, also, I have rediscovered the value of my heritage. Perhaps it is a case of not being able to see the forest for the trees. Perhaps it is the reopening of the conduits of perception and love that had atrophied under the constant disdain in the gaze of so many Southern Baptists. I don't know.

I do know that neither Joe nor I fled to any gay Mecca to become openly queer. For good or ill, each of us spent his youth and formative queer years within the comfort and confines of familiar dialects and landscapes. We were not alone. Many gay people were locked into our particular corner of the world. It may be less remarkable now, but in the 1970s and 1980s, it wasn't the stuff of literature. Joe and I both followed our bliss the relatively short distance to the beach, which itself played a historical role in each of our families.

Both Joe and I are from families who were American before there was an America. From Dorset and Devon, England, our progenitors arrived here in the hundred years before the Revolution. Beguiled by some sense of vague promise, some desperation or need unfulfilled in England, they sailed for the colonies. Tidewater Virginia and Carolina have kept their long-agreed-upon, intuited, but unstated promises with our forebears. Those promises held both of us for much of our adult lives.

This is a phenomenon that many people do not understand about Southerners. They groan and roll their eyes in anticipation of another Faulknerian opus full of centuries-old feuds, madness, and a homegrown form of ancestor worship. The simple truth is nowhere near that predictable. Newer Americans, the rootless children of contemporary carpetbaggers and those who define home only by the location of the homogenized glow from a television screen, can have no empathy for the experience of home. Not as we know it.

It is difficult to explain to a non-Southerner this physical and spiritual attachment to a place. I am rarely homesick in the sense that people often define the experience. I have no nostalgic longing for a past place. I often feel as though going back to North Carolina is to experience some odd time-space disjunct. It is as if I board a plane in Fort Lauderdale only to arrive, in ninety minutes' time, back in 1962. That disjunct is more a factor of the resident's mind-set than the physical surroundings.

I feel an almost physical need for the sight of broad marshes, for long fields of corn or tobacco, and for the shallow sound waters stretching under the colder light of a more northern parallel. I long sometimes for a slate-colored sea, even as I swim in the turquoise sea of Florida. That place's hold on me and on my imagination demands an odd kind of loyalty.

It is lonesome to betray that loyalty. Joe never has. His world's orbit has remained successfully within a two-hundred-mile radius of his birthplace. By right, tradition, and expectation, so should have mine. But that was not to be, at least not yet. The reach of Tidewater to gather in its children is both long and very patient.

During a visit to my parents' home a couple of years ago, my dad produced a family history that had been carefully researched by a near cousin. Much to my dad's amusement and some satisfaction, the family history revealed much about the founder of our clan. Born in England, the many-great grandfather migrated first to Providence, Rhode Island. He worked as a whaler and a boatbuilder. Becoming successful, he moved along to Beaufort, North Carolina, to marry the daughter of the local Anglican minister. Part of her dowry was the northern end of Davis Island. This is now called Core Banks and is part of the Cape Hatteras National Seashore.

My dad is retired from a thirty-year career with the Department of Defense. Only a few days shy of his eighteenth birthday, he decided that the life of a tenant farmer on someone else's land wasn't any kind of life he wanted. The youngest son of a deceased father and dependent of his eldest brother, he waited out his mother's refusal to sign for him to join the Air Force prior to his birthday. The day he turned eighteen, he signed up.

He completed basic training in Cheyenne, Wyoming. He spent his years in the Air Force in Washington, DC. Leaving the Air Force, he made a civilian career of working in the Department of Defense. His job took him from eastern North Carolina to Guam. He retired, with my mother, to Bogue Banks. My dad returned to within a few miles of where the family had been launched centuries before.

Joe's father, like mine, was a younger son of a very large farm family. Unlike my father, Joe's family owned the land they farmed. In our fathers' generation, children were still bred for labor as much as out of love, and the traditions of primogeniture and the simple facts of a farm's carrying capacity created the harsh reality that the younger sons had to seek a livelihood away from home.

Joe Riddick senior faced the same hard option as my father. With a strong back and some skill, he left his Gates County, North Carolina, homestead to join the Navy. Also, as with my father, the military provided the next step up. World War II and the Korean War offered many Tidewater boys like our fathers the chance to get somewhere on their own. The military was college and graduate school for them.

Unlike my father, Joe's dad left the military after the war. He began a construction business that grew successfully in proportion to his burgeoning family. When he died, too soon, in the mid-1980s, he had made his life in Suffolk, Virginia. He passed away within a few miles of the mansion called Riddick's Folly near the Suffolk riverfront, which had been built by his own forebear who began the dynasty Joe's daddy had continued.

Perhaps now one can begin to understand the deep and long conversation that Southern land shares in whispers with all its sons, even the queer ones. In the face of so long a tradition, so predictable a path, how could we leave? How could we stay? The land lets you leave, but it never lets you go. Your existence is inextricably linked with the past, no matter how at odds your sexual identity is with it.

This existence, as it was and as it is still, continues somewhere. The context is only specifically Southern in its locus and gay in its incarnation. Joe and I both grew up tow-headed and scabby-kneed in backyards ubiquitous in their ordinariness.

This ordinary existence only began to disintegrate for both of us, and for the rest of the world, in the 1960s. The old traditions of the agrarian South began to shift to encompass broader concepts of society and personal choice. The social fabric of our world became tattered, as old identities and relationships stretched and broke as society strained toward another decade. Black people demanded to be heard. Women collectively argued to be recognized. Southern queers began to exercise their resolve against being beaten into invisibility. The bills of so many years of tradition came due. Ignorance and bigotry grew unfashionable and retreated to the Assembly of God to await their reawakening as religious conservatism in the 1990s.

People began to "relate" to one another as individuality came into vogue. Our mothers and fathers, brothers and sisters began to flex their own identities. Our fathers grew sideburns and prosperous midsections. Our mothers raised their hemlines and their consciousness. After centuries of subsumed needs to the tyranny of social convention and common need, the individual raised its long-humbled head and hollered, "What about me?" Indeed, what about me? What about Joe? We followed this current, as an ominous, bitten-back understanding crept through our perceptions of life.

We each began to understand that our own quest for this precious new identity would carry this sudden apostasy to a new level. We knew we would never grow up to marry and make a new generation. The 1960s performed a most amazing sleight of hand with us. We would become the fringe of all those hard-won new freedoms. While the world around us tested the thickness of tolerance in careful steps, it was up to us to rush onto the ice.

In our headlong embrace of our own identities, we dragged our families and our world along with us. All of us were growing up. The long-standing conversation with a landscape and a way of life on it dwindled in the rush for self-satisfaction. No family was immune. We all came through the years between the mid-1960s and the mid-1990s individually. Only our own collective dynamics with one another remained unchanged.

Thinking about what creates such strong family ties among gay men in general and between me and Joe in particular must begin with what is shared in common. If you believe in the uniquely Americanized version of reincarnation, this could explain the rush of kinship and delight in another's company. If you are only a realist, you could find cold comfort in the notion that people bond simply as a result of proximity and common interest.

I think that being Southern born provides a shared vocabulary, visual and verbal, that can create a twin language in the unrelated sons of the Tidewater plain.

Chapter 3

Family by Blood

Gelatin silver emulsion is the genetic material of memory for me. In the images captured and transformed by light floating on their surface is the great record of my life. I most love the old black-and-white snapshots from my earliest childhood. I keep several framed in my guest room. One is of my father and me seated on a large paper moon in Carolina Beach. I was two. He was twenty-nine. Looking at it, I feel as singular as my fingerprint, but still as much a part of my father as his own fingerprint. Blood memory. Gelatin silver prints.

In that bedroom, I keep another set of pictures that means a great deal to me. The set is a series of my mother and father, each picture taken on a beach, marking different intervals of their life together. The first was taken on one of their first dates. They pose, in hopelessly period swimsuits, leaning against a 1949 Ford. In this image of them together, I begin to see myself as the hybrid of them both, long before there was a me, or even much of a them.

My dad mugs at the anonymous photographer, boyishly brash. My mom rolls her eyes at some unknown point in the middle distance, her arms folded under her bathing suit's pointy bosom. Doe-eyed and dark-haired, my mom has a no-nonsense stance compared to my dad's loose-limbed slouch. Seriousness met and married happy self-assurance.

My mom told me once that she loved coming to visit my house because it was the only place in the world that had pictures of her on the wall. But then again, my home is also a familiar place to her and my father because it is kept by someone they made together. Those old photographs carry her memories forward—as I carry her and my father forward.

This is where we begin to find out who we are. A photograph carries not only the image of the subject but an image of an environment and a point in time. Now older than the people were when those photographs were taken, I see my younger self.

On the desk in his den, Joe has a picture of his father taken when Joe senior was in the Navy. He was a good-looking squid, staring out of the frame, frozen forever in that instant between boy and man, his grin maturing from boyish bravado to manly self-assurance. I have a picture of my own father taken when he was approximately the same age as Joe senior in his photo. Coltish and pretty, he shares the transitional grin and a face unmarked by the responsibilities that would gnaw at them both as time went by.

Joe looks more like his father as he matures. He has the same height and build. He has the same inner balance. Joe told me not long ago that he caught a glimpse of a man and, for a moment, was taken aback. The man looked so much like his father that he felt a simultaneous rush of disbelief and longing. The man turned out to be Joe himself, tricked by a reflection in a mirror.

I find my father staring back at me unexpectedly from the mirror as well. Sometimes, I open my mouth and my father's words in his tone of voice jump out, surprising me much as my dogs were surprised when they learned to bark. For a moment, they would look around frightened, not yet aware that they were the source of the sound. In addition to his voice, I am acquiring my father's frame. I already have his chin, and I never cease looking for the sparkle of his green eyes in my hazel ones.

For Joe and me, time and this age reveal our deep connection with the men who made us. Our fathers created us physically and gifted us with a variety of attributes that they willingly allowed others to nurture. Joe and I were born in the 1950s. Then, real men bred the kids and left the details of their upbringing to their wives. Like feudal lords, they ran their fiefdoms, meted out discipline, and set policy. But they also built the walls and lowered the portcullis between us and intimate knowledge of them. Intimacy was for mamas.

Only now do we find such intimacy with our fathers, by their example and in our own reflections. My dad is generally a quiet man, but he'll tell you to go to hell in a hot minute if you push him hard enough. So will I. I find I have become my father's child in the middle of my life. Joe exercises the same reasoned judgment his father always did, but it is attached to a shorter fuse than his father ever possessed. We both come to this intimacy with our fathers through a familiar filter, our mothers.

Looking at those grinning boys in their photographs, bleached pewter with time, you can understand their appeal to a certain type of woman. Their grins had a teasing, challenging quality. Their eyes held a promise of heat but hinted at a cool steeliness just beneath the surface. It would take a formidable young woman to accept the challenge offered by those eyes and knowing grins. That's what both men got.

My parents married when my mom was just shy of her nineteenth birthday and my dad was twenty-two. They immediately assumed a maturity that I managed to avoid until I was almost thirty. They made a commitment to each other that I couldn't replicate until I was thirty-three. Looking at them as young people from the august distance of my own middle age, I marvel at their achievement in sustaining both a marriage and an abiding affection for almost fifty years. I also envy the support and succor provided by the age that formed them.

Joe's parents' marriage followed a similar pattern. His mom was fifteen and his dad twenty-one when they married. They shared a life together that was as much an achievement over rough beginnings as it was a testament to simple love. Joe's mom and dad, like my own, worked to provide freedom from the same harsh economic options they faced. Like others of the age, they worked diligently to provide their children with a leg up in the world through college and middle-class surroundings.

If questioned, I don't think either my parents or Joe's would define themselves as middle class, at least not in the way we view that category today. When one is living a life, it is almost impossible to step outside of it to define it. Our parents were more apt to subscribe to a theory of existence that is particularly Southern in context: their lives were guided by the notion of *doing right*.

Doing right encompassed every nuance of our parents' lives. Their essentially Protestant and puritanical religion tinted every action, in the abstract and in practice. For a man to do right, he had to hold a job, take care of his family through several generations, and participate in some way in the broader life of his church and community. To be a man, he had to be discreet in his indiscretions and appear to be strong in the face of the worst the world could throw at him.

For a woman to do right, she had to abandon her individuality to her husband first, her children second, and her church finally. To be a real woman, she had to breed and she had to persevere, and she had to do so with a loyalty that transcended and abrogated any sense of self. Self-expression was limited to cooking, home, and children. Her children were her handicraft and her career. Every unwiped, snotty nose, every thrown stone or showing slip was an indictment of her ability to do right. Every good report card, every child's trip to the dentist cavity-free, and every child's clean appearance at Sunday school were her validation.

Our parents were scrutinized by the generation preceding them, and by their own, constantly. The glue that bound their entire world together was a presumed and overwhelming sense of surveillance. I remember being a kid, running around with my dad or in the grocery store with my mom. We'd encounter some distant relative or near acquaintance and ask, "How you doing? And your folks, they doing all right?"

The old friend or cousin would murmur modestly, "Oh, yeah. Doing fine, doing fine." We'd hear of old so-and-so who wasn't doing too good. Sympathetic, we'd respond with the news of that sorry somebody who wasn't doing right by his wife, or who was down sick. We'd hear of someone else who finally did right by his daddy, or of the poor unfortunate who couldn't do *nothing* right. Reassured of our own and everyone else's performance on that great "do right" scale, we'd say "Bye" and pass on.

This was the measure our parents took of themselves and the world around them. The individual cost must have been taxing to the point of exhaustion. In so many ways, they deconstructed themselves and then built themselves again into the identities demanded by their world. In buttoning themselves into this constriction, they willingly traded personal need, always viewed as sheer selfishness, for those things which mattered—children, church, community.

Those words are written large in cartoonish strokes in politics and religious circles today. In our parents' time, there was no discussion of "Family Values," no jingoistic reduction of the practical business of existence as it had been patterned since time began. Our parents had no lifestyle choices. Either you did right, or you didn't.

Life stages for them were clearly mapped. I would dismiss them as mere breeder automatons marching in lockstep through predictable lives, but I cannot. I was a witness to the sheer effort it took them to create a meaningful life together, and to the many who failed where they succeeded. I also carry the expectation, one that life created in Joe and me, for a close and loving partnership with another person.

As an adage, the apple doesn't fall too far from the tree didn't earn its reputation as a shibboleth for no reason. Living for eighteen years in an atmosphere of love, with daily examples of the practice of marriage, created in both Joe and me a hunger to re-create that atmosphere in our own lives. Our early environment gave us the tools to create and maintain a marriage; it did not, however, give us permission to do so for many years, nor did it ensure success or re-creation of our parents' lives for our siblings.

Both Joe's parents and mine created their families through passion and accident. I was the oldest of three children. Joe is a middle child of six. With predictable regularity, our parents heeded the biblical command to go forth, be fruitful, and multiply. In doing so, they fulfilled the first criterion of doing right. Children are the raison d'être.

Daddies work so their children can have a roof over their heads and biscuits on the table. Daddies tithe so that their children can be brought up in a church that provides an ethical framework for a community. Mamas do right by keeping their young'uns clean and teaching them to respect their daddies. Mamas work hard to prepare the food daddies put on the table. They carpool and make cookies for bake sales and Scout trips.

Children do right by honoring their daddies and mamas. They behave and look after their brothers and sisters. They go to school to learn so they can perpetuate the strides the family has taken away from rough starts and cruel twists of fate. All of this was part and parcel of the environment into which Joe and I were born.

Strict adherence to the path our parents had trudged before us knit us into that whole *do right* attitude. We joined our place in line or on the church pew to hear the promises of that culture. While the promises were stingy at times and their keeping seemed to come only in glimpses, we joined the larger community through our families and our churches.

Our parents buying into that narrow path earned us an introduction into a broader world. Because of who they were and what they did, we inherited an initial identity and place in the scheme of things. Our place in the feudal landscape was ensured.

With the inheritance of that place, the surveillance began. With the admonition from our parents to "be sweet," which really meant "behave" or "obey," we learned to say "Yes, Sir," and "Yes, Ma'am." Those lessons were so ingrained that thirty-odd years later I still use those addresses when speaking to anyone in authority, even those obviously my junior. We learned that no actions of our own were ours alone. Everything we did was a direct reflection of our parents.

Joe tells a story of how he was caught speeding on the way to school one morning. He was held to account for his behavior in his father's office that night. It had taken less than an hour for his father to learn of his transgression.

When in high school myself, I once went to Greensboro to a LaBelle concert (the "Wear Something Silver Tour"). My best friend and running buddy was already a freshman at Greensboro College. We spent the Saturday afternoon before the concert gluing hundreds of single sequins on our skin and clothing. That night, he led me into War Memorial Auditorium on an aluminum chain-link leash and a choke collar. Despite Greensboro being three hours away, our brief nod to S&M chic was reported to his parents, then mine. I recall now, with no small amount of glee, the reflection my bare sixteen-year-old, silver-spangled torso must have cast to catch some disapproving eye more than two hundred miles down Highway 70. By that time, the notion of doing right was stretched a little thin for me.

I was not alone. Joe and I both began to grope for identities that were not so dictated by formula, as our fathers withdrew into themselves. Wearied by a world they defined as "dog eat dog," their deep wells of testosterone dwindled to provide only enough aggression to maintain our and our siblings' insatiable thirst for cars, education, and clothes.

Our mothers threw themselves outward into a broader world than found in the kitchen and within the church's boundaries. Our brothers and sisters wrestled with the twin chimeras of love and career. Our familial links became forged more from shared gene pools and less from affection and proximity. Our familial responsibilities became parodies of the pure form we expressed as younger parents and children.

Joe's mother read his personal letters looking for evidence that he was gay. When she found it, she resolved to cure him of this threat to her esteem. She, in all love and earnestness, believed that she could pit her will against his personality, as though she were attempting some advanced form of potty training. She found a doctor who practiced aversion therapy. He would do right if it killed him. Joe successfully pleaded against the doctor's genital torture and his mother's determination to have hime "cured."

My mother told me that she knew I was gay. A psychiatrist who presided over my very nontraditional crack-up at age ten predicted it. She cringed at her own intelligent understanding that she could do nothing. For the first time in our lives, our mothers perceived that we had done something they couldn't fix or change. Resignation grew in their hearts, slowly bearing the fruit of acceptance.

At the admission of homosexuality, Joe's dad never stopped loving him or isolated him in any way. My dad shook his head as if struck by a blow he'd expected to avoid but he quickly recovered and our relationship remained the same.

Our fathers regarded us with a mixture of amusement, bewilderment, and curious pride, as if we were bright and alien glimmers, shimmering perpetually just beyond the corners of their eyes. For all their rough-handed affection in their efforts to rear us to be men, they had created, surprisingly, some special hybrid that was all man, yet curiously free from all the weight and responsibility of manhood as they lived it.

A man may become a father, but he remains a boy in some sense all his life. Boys are self-centered and self-involved above all else. In their drive for maturity, they often acquire the very trappings of ambition and aggression that bury the boy under layers of responsibility. In the love and affection given us by our fathers after the admission of our queerness, I find evidence of our fathers' amusement that we beat the system.

As for regrets, I would not trivialize the disappointment our fathers must have felt on a personal level. The hunger for progeny doesn't leave a man after he's produced his own offspring. Joe's dad saw grandchildren from Joe's siblings long before he died. My father will not be so lucky. A variety of circumstances precluded that particular satisfaction for him.

From neither Joe's dad nor my own did I ever feel a sense of failure on their part for our sexual identity. Both were very successful men in terms of how their communities judged their ability to do right. Our queerness did not reflect poorly on them. Their hard-won sense of self would never permit it. What their sense of self did allow is a certain undiluted pride in our stubbornness and self-assertion. There is a fine line, after all, between beating your will into a son and beating the spirit out of him.

My dad's father was a son of a bitch. He truly beat his children. What is called child abuse now was called discipline then. Of course, my grandfather's father was just as bad. Hard times required them to be hard men. I recall meeting an old man one day with my father. The old man had been a county sheriff for many years before his retirement. He recounted an ambush my grandfather and his father set up to shoot a neighbor with whom they had some issue. A certain amount of gunfire was exchanged, but no one was killed.

Although my dad grew up that way, he decided to raise his young'uns a different way. Having been beaten, he chose not to beat us. Despite his firm, but gentler discipline, I still have a vestigial redneck gene from my grandfather. I see a certain grin of recognition when telling my father about my ability to handle the bullshit that comes my way. A certain amount of personality comes undiluted from older sources. I recall my dad's laughter when I sang to him a lyric from a Lyle Lovett song, "Redneck-ness must be a disease. You get a little on your fingers and it crawls up your sleeves." Congenital or contagious, in me, this heritage of redneck tenacious pugnacity lurks just under a thin skin of civility.

The inheritance of a Southern male isn't invalidated by homosexuality. I presume by his tolerance that Joe's dad must have shared my father's feelings when he said, "Well, son, you got a hard row to hoe, but life ain't easy on nobody." Our fathers dealt with our queerness by judging our ability to do right in a difficult set of circumstances. That is something they could relate to with an understanding passed along for generations.

Our mamas were a different matter. Our mamas bent pieces of their own iron will into backbones for every one of their children, gay or straight. Despite that effort, our mothers never really trusted our ability to use that backbone, even when we used it to assert ourselves as gay men.

It is difficult to surrender the absolute control of a benevolent dictatorship that begins prior to our individual consciousness. How do you go from switching the legs of a disobedient toddler to mere benign chastisement of the adult? How do you go from being a savior to a mildly interested bystander?

If you are Joe's mama or mine, you don't. One Christmas, my partner Jeff made a broad joke at my expense in the company of both our families. I blew it off as no big deal. Our Christmas Eve proceeded pleasantly through dinner and on to Midnight Mass. Convoying to church in separate cars, I realized that my mother was furious. She had taken great offense at Jeff's joke. She said, "I will put your little ass in my car and carry you home if that's the way he treats you. Ain't nobody gonna talk about my young'un that way and get away with it."

My mother needed some reassurance on my part, and my father's, that she was making much of nothing. My mother actually adores Jeff. He is the recipient of every unreserved part of her affection. Still, an offhand remark was enough to rouse the watchful mother-lioness instinct. I admit to feeling an unalloyed sense of security, even as an adult, in that protectiveness. "My mama don't play."

Neither does Joe's mama. When I first met him, Joe worked for the business that his mother had started. Never really comfortable with Joe's expression of affection toward men, his mother regarded me with undisguised distaste that strained her Southern lady training to be polite at all costs. Whenever I called Joe at work or appeared in person, she treated me with brusque politeness that burned worse than an outright slap.

No matter how hard I plied my charm and deference to warm her icy reception, I was always met with a chilly condescension usually reserved for white trash or ex-cons. One day, fed up with the freeze out, I seized an unlikely opportunity that found the two of us alone together. I told her, in no uncertain terms, that I was Joe's friend, but I was not sleeping with him, so she didn't have any reason to treat me like some slut after his money or something. I concluded my little heart-to-heart talk by telling her I was a good friend, and since he didn't have that many, she'd be doing him a favor not to run me off with her attitude.

I think the long thaw began after she got her breath back. Nonetheless, I have spent less time wooing lovers than I have earning Joe's mother's affection. I suppose, for that reason, I value it more than I do the less-hard-won good humor of many others. In the years following that confrontation, Joe's mother has opened her home to give me refuge from a hurricane; she's fed me and followed my ups and downs with all the concern of a surrogate parent. Once you have made it into a lioness's heart, you have a place there for life.

The maintenance on that place can be costly, however. I don't think there is a man alive who can't relate to Alexander the Great's lament on reading a letter from his mother. He is said to have cried, "God, that woman charges high rent on the nine months' lodging she gave me." Women raise their sons with a gusto born of their own presumed ability both to correct the father's flaws and to make a man for a man's world. Ultimately, they are left bereft and lonely in the wake of their successful efforts.

My mother once said that the umbilical cord between mothers and sons is cut with dull, rusty scissors. She never said whose hands held them. Our mothers reared us to be little soldiers, forgetting that soldiers don't cry and they don't come home for long periods of time. So our mothers court us unabashedly. They admire us without reservation and wrap us in extravagant praise. When that fails to elicit an appropriate response, our mothers can become critical and judgmental. They can become icily distant and tearfully hurt. At times their emotions are bruised by the very effort of extending them for our acknowledgment.

More with my straight brother than with me, I see this scene between mother and son repeated over and over. It leaves him in a state of weary bewilderment. Somehow, whatever he seems to proffer emotionally, it is never enough.

Sons, gay or straight, operate on the concept of out of sight, out of mind. Unless a need presents itself, whining and panting in front of their faces, their absorption with the tasks at hand precludes any perception of a need. Thus, mothers endlessly court their grown sons. They constantly feel stood up for a date their sons never knew they had.

Although my former ability to accurately view the dynamics of Joe's family has been diminished by physical distance, I have seen evidence of this same pattern in the past. Periods of estrangement and gruff reunion occurred between Joe's brothers (and sisters) and their mother. As in much else, watching Joe's evolving relationships with his mother and his siblings informed my actions when my own life stages began to mimic his.

From Joe, I learned the secrets of family maintenance. It involves empathy first, then forgiveness. In some ways, empathy is the easiest to achieve. It takes little more than meeting the responsibilities that come with a job, a lease, a mortgage, and a marriage, of sorts. The only difficulty with empathy is the time it takes to come to it. Empathy only comes with some measure of maturity, with some emotional wear and tear.

Forgiveness is more difficult. Without forgiveness, however, it is impossible to achieve an emotionally self-supporting adulthood. A family is as much an accumulation of hurts and slights as it is an accretion of happier shared experiences. Amazingly, much of family dynamics seems to be based on personally cherished grudges. As evidenced in Joe's family and in my own, it is impossible to sustain a strong sense of family without coming to terms with the sibling who always got the biggest piece of chicken or the woman who had to teach you to pee standing up.

I count myself lucky to have blood family who have become my friends. Joe shares a comparable level of fortune with his mother, brothers, and sisters. It would be naive to assume that everyone else is as fortunate. States of benign neglect and open warfare are how many of my friends describe their "relationships" with their blood families. Despite the enmity that exists in these definitions of family, there does seem to be a great deal of comfort in conflict for them. A family's abiding connection can be maintained by shared conflict or comfort.

Our own strengths and weaknesses are mirrored in varying degrees in our brothers and sisters. Through a long blood communication, we possess an intimacy with and perception of them that jells our own identities. In Joe's larger family and his middle place in it, I have witnessed shifting alliances and rivalries of Byzantine complexity. I have also seen accommodations made and boundaries drawn and redrawn between them that have shifted and settled into a family foundation that is not static, but still elemental.

Joe grew up being third in line after two brothers who were "A" students and sports heroes. Despite their stair-step appearance in age and looks, his older brothers refused to allow anyone to paint the three of them with the same brush. Joe was the "talented" one, and his brothers vigorously defended his right to his own identity. They maintained that defense even as it developed along lines that rapidly diverged from their own.

As they grew older, Joe's divergence from their predictable social and sexual patterns created silences and distances, which his burgeoning sexual persona as a gay man lengthened and deepened. Despite that estrangement, an abiding brotherly love still made itself known—but in actions, not in words.

Joe experienced few direct confrontations or emotional outbursts. In a sense, it was as if Joe's identity in the family became defined in relation to his brothers' and sisters' identities. As their identities were confirmed by marriages and the steady production of children, Joe's identity was confirmed in contrast.

Sibling bonds are created more in deed than in conversation. It is part and parcel of a Southern upbringing to be stoic and old-time tough in relegating personal problems, and even joy, to the private realm. Although much camaraderie exists after the fact, during the actual event that code requires you to walk alone. Every sibling is given the slack necessary to make his or her own mistakes or successes. It is a matter of respect not to meddle in your brother's business, even if you suspect that he's getting himself into a mess.

Years after the fact, I learned that one of Joe's older brothers had received word from a Dare County law enforcement officer that Joe was hanging out with some bad company. That bad company was me. Joe's brother casually mentioned to him what he had been told and, without judgment or condemnation, advised him to be careful. From that particular brother, or from any other for that matter, I never got one cross word or long sideways look. It seemed enough that I was Joe's friend. The same latitude they extended to their brother, they extended to me.

I survived my drug years, got out of them in fact, primarily because of Joe's friendship and influence. So many years later, I am grateful for the latitude Joe's family gave me and for the trust they had in their brother to choose his own friends. A family as large and tight as Joe's must feel a great deal of goodwill for one another to extend that acceptance to the friends of the family.

The Riddick family is by no means perfect, with rivalries and grudges among the siblings that rise and fall with all the intensity of the weather. What does remain, under such transitory irritations, is a remarkable acceptance of one another. Blood family is a constant, for good or ill, with only gray areas in between. I have lived in and out of gray weather in that regard myself.

I grew up with two younger brothers. Within three years of meeting Joe, I lost the middle brother to a sudden and particularly virulent form of cancer. It took me a long time to understand that not everything was about me. Finding my own family suddenly diminished by 20 percent left me wobbly and uncertain as to my role as a vital part of what remained.

While I always loved, and more important respected, my brothers, it was my tendency to relegate them to walk-on roles in the great drama of my life. Selfishly and stupidly absorbed in reaching my own goals, I neglected to appreciate their dramas, both great and small. Capriciously alternating between being a bully and a bad-ass, I was every ugly metaphor for an older brother. I related to my brothers with brief flashes of generosity in a broad sky of selfish arrogance. Larger and smarter by right of age, I ruled over them with a doggy psychology of dominance.

With perception sharpened now by distance, one brother having died and the other living nine hundred miles away, I can see they gave me the same latitude that Joe's brothers and sisters always gave him. Early on, I think they must have seen past the cold distance I created between us and loved me despite it.

My middle brother, too soon dead, had a way of cutting through my histrionics with keen insight and a sense of humor that I sorely miss. My baby brother, very much alive and very much appreciated now, has a way of lumping me together with my mother that is maddening, but very intuitive, and often, very correct. He has lived with me long enough to have seen my arrogance humbled and my pretensions unmasked for the puffery they always were. Despite that, he still gives me respect I never really earned and affection I've taken for granted.

It couldn't have been easy for either of my brothers to follow behind my lead. Unlike Joe, they didn't have an "A" student or sports hero role model to follow. I spent many of my years at home as a manic depressive. The collective wisdom of psychiatry available in eastern North Carolina in the early 1960s through the mid-1970s did not believe in the childhood onset of manic-depressive disorder. My brothers thus grew up with a volatility on the part of their older brother that defied explanation.

Going down memory lane during a visit to my parents' home, my baby brother took a detour to the time I taught him a dance called "The Muscle." I had the Parliament-Funkadelic album with "Flashlight" on it. We hooked it up on the big floor model stereo that Mama and Daddy had in the living room and played that song over and over as I taught him the dance.

Our poor daddy was used to a fifteen-minute nap before supper. With the unmistakable opening strains of "Flashlight" beginning for the umpteenth time, he hollered from his easy chair in the den, "Ya'll turn that shit OFF! Ain't you heard *washcloth* about seventy times by now?" More than twenty years later, recalling our father's unhip irritation and poor hearing still brings a great deal of laughter. I remembered dancing all the time back then. My brother said, with a grin, "Yeah, if you weren't dancing, you were bitching or raising hell about something."

Those were the twin poles of my existence. I moved between intense manic activity and vicious exasperation born of exhaustion, with no break in between. The demands I placed on my family were just as extreme. I perpetuated a state of crisis in our household that became my brothers' norm.

Doggedly, my brothers took all kinds of abuse that my erratic behavior and bizarre persona drew from their larger world. For them, my coming out was no more or less a hardship or an accommodation than anything else I had thrown at them. Somehow, through blood ties or an astounding sense of loyalty, they gave me a love that was ungrudging and constant.

Interestingly, I have learned that my partner, Jeff, also an eldest child, exhibited the same irritability and combativeness in his family that I did. His actions never went off the deep end, but they did result in some busted sheetrock. Now, as adults, we have fallen in together, each seeming to have met his match. My brother and his wife are both youngest children. Jeff's middle brother's wife is also a middle child, and his youngest brother is partnered with a youngest child.

Although opposites attract, it does seem true that likes stay together. At the very least, you go with what you know. Joe's partner, Brad, is both some years younger than Joe and a youngest child to Joe's middle birth order. As he has done throughout his life, Joe has found someone with whom to re-create a family that is most familiar.

So our blood families determine the dynamics of our families of choice. They foreshadow the latitude we extend and are extended as we choose lovers and friends who become brothers. The long dialogue of gay brothers of choice begins on a common soil and extends itself to the community through the family. It begins as an unspoken sense of kinship that encourages the conversation and sustains it throughout, acknowledging the bond without blood.

For Joe and me, the similarity of our backgrounds and experiences made empathy inevitable. What extended empathy into a longer series of life lessons? Joe was used to helping his younger siblings along. When I appeared, it was an opportunity for him to grow beyond a big brother role and exercise his accumulated wisdom in the form of a surrogate parent.

For all my carefully crafted sense of self, I was still a feral gay child. I had all of the instinct, but none of the direction that melds instinct into socialization. I matured astoundingly under Joe's parentage in terms of becoming an "out" gay person. Joe provided the sense of stability and unconditional support that allowed me to take my first tentative steps into gay life.

If an introduction to gay life and benevolent supervision of my burgeoning gay identity were all that Joe's parentage accomplished, that would have been a great thing. However, a child can grow into a healthy adult with only bread and water, and its emotional nutritional equivalent, from a blood parent. Joe's parentage/mentoring role for me extended beyond the practical lessons of queerdom. He gave me a sense of living that life in the whole, big world.

In our blood homes and families we are socialized into a broader application of our identities. Our contexts of class, ethnicity, culture, and ethical systems are fed to us as certainly as actual nourishment. From Joe, I learned what it was to be gay in the small and large world in which I lived. I learned a sense of appropriateness and ethics from a gay context.

I watched Joe square his shoulders and through his actions announce to clients, community leaders, blood family, and friends that his identity as a gay man was not negotiable. Joe taught me that it was fundamentally dishonest to try to "pass" for straight. It takes backbone to never compromise on a hard-won identity. In many ways, I climbed up Joe's backbone to commit personally and publicly to my own identity as a gay man.

Chapter 4

Recovering Baptists

The differences between Joe's family and my own are mainly ones of geography, age, and number. We share strong siblings and stronger parents. We have shared a time and place, and the growing pains common to that time. The overriding source of comfort and pain in our similarities stems not from a common queerness but from the foundation of our world, the Southern Baptist Church.

I will not say that our parents had us in church every time they cracked open the door, but I wouldn't be exaggerating to say they came close. There was Sunday school and Sunday morning worship. There was Training Union and Sunday evening worship every Sunday night. Wednesday was prayer meeting and choir practice. The other nights of the week could be consumed by deacon's meeting, Ladies Auxiliary, and Home Missions. Each summer was Vacation Bible School, and at least quarterly, there was Revival.

Growing up, it never ceased to puzzle me why we Baptists needed Revival for something we never ceased doing. The answer lay in the long-standing conversation between the people and the flat Tidewater landscape they inhabited. Life was hard there. It was a capricious existence coaxing crops from its dark soil or pulling fish from its sounds and waters. Children of farmers and fishermen knew the tenuous line between success and starvation. Rains could come too often or not often enough. Hurricanes could manifest without warning to down crops and sink boats. There were malarial summers and bitter winters. They owed everything, including daily survival, to God's grace.

The God of the Southern Baptists is the God of Abraham. He is a vengeful and judging God, prone in his displeasure to chastise his children with the mindless heavy-handed justice of an irritable granddaddy coming off a three-day drunk. Our mothers and fathers understood that God. In many ways, he was the personification of their own fathers, who unflinchingly shot sick dogs and slit hogs' throats.

Our parents' fathers beat the living shit out of them for their own good when they disobeyed. They did this not out of meanness, but from a certainty that they were doing what they had to do. How could our parents, and their parents all the way back to England, expect Almighty God to do any less?

They loved God's son, Jesus, while they mistrusted his gentleness. Jesus was too selfless for them. He was too forgiving for a people whose only inheritance was grudges and deep class and racial hatred. These people could only love the Son of God abstractly. They loved and feared his father instinctively. He demanded of them complete and total obedience, conformity, and devotion. For that, he gave them his son as comforter, but he spared them nothing in his random violence and casual disregard.

It took Revival to keep them in line. It was a cathartic and cleansing spiritual ass-whupping. The unending threat of damnation helped to sweeten the starkness of their redemption. Revival reassured them they were doing right. Doing right made the crops grow and kept the fish biting. It kept your young'uns from laziness, and the hunger to rise above their station. It kept your wife or husband out of the tuberculosis ward. It was an old promise from an old Promised Land.

Southern Baptists of that time needed one another's company to protect them from the assaults of a world that was rapidly educating them away from the collective bicameral mind in which the sect flourished. Present-day Southern Baptists function in much the same way, despite a tentative flirtation with education and a certain touchy-feely psychological approach to salvation.

Primal superstition aside, what are the various Christian sects or, indeed, religions of any stripe? They are basically institutions that exist primarily to indoctrinate children into an ethical belief system. They function as a type of club for people who agree to share a particular expression of worship. They form a social support network for all members of the club regardless of age or social position. These sects provide a context for existence from cradle to grave.

That narrow definition leaves little room for the lively experience of being a Southern Baptist, or a Catholic or a Jew, for that matter. There is the squirming of your little brother as you pinch the hell out of him as he sits on the hard pew, swinging his legs in boredom; the clean smell of starch in your daddy's freshly ironed shirt as he stretches his arm across the back of the pew, letting you sleep against his side until the pastor calls for the final hymn; the rapt gaze of your mother as her mind seeks blessed assurance in the droning words of the sermon; the slow but sure dull wit of the heavy lady across the aisle as she vigorously nods at each of the sermon's three points.

In these experiences is commonality, but also fear and distrust, which are as readily extended to members when they step out of line, intellectually or socially, as is the comfort of community in times of need. Both Joe and I stepped out of line, first, at the impetus of our intelligence and, finally, at the insistence of our identities as gay men.

The aggressive ignorance of the Southern Baptist dogma refuses to acknowledge its queer children or even the possibility that they could sprout from its congregation. Of course, there is that organist or choir director who is a little funny, but he's awful good to his mama and he keeps the prettiest yard in town. It doesn't even register to the congregation that they live their whole lives in simplistic duplicity. The queer part of the Southern Baptist Church can be found easily in the rest stops along major interstates and in certain bathrooms throughout the region, but you won't find it in church on Sunday morning.

Hypocrisy is not solely the possession of the Southern Baptists, but they have made themselves into its broadest caricature. It is a common enough joke to say that Baptists are like cats: you know they're out raising hell, but you just can't catch them at it. The point is that they are so self-deluded they cannot even admit to being caught. As quick as they have ever been to cry crocodile tears at the admission of their own sinfulness, they are stingy with any understanding of personal growth. They are far less ready to embrace God with their minds than they are with their faith.

Bashing Southern Baptists is rather like beating a mule that stubbornly plants its hooves and merely lowers its head under the blows. Presumably, Southern Baptists conceded that the earth was round and, exhausted by that intellectual stretch, planted their collective hooves to await Armageddon.

It would be easy to dismiss them if there weren't so damn many of them. As individuals, they work with and buy from gay people. They even call some of them friends. Yet, with a violent wrenching of their consciences, they, as a group, can call for civil injustice and persecution of the same people with whom they knowingly interact on a daily basis. Long accustomed to Jim Crow laws, they have extended them de facto to the gay population since the black population threw off the de jure fact. This capability for transference is what makes them so scary.

Politically, Southern Baptists have learned well the lessons of Joseph Goebbels. The best way to exterminate a population is to demonize and dehumanize it as a group. Jews and homosexuals both met death in the Nazi concentration camps. One cannot help but shudder at the potential for violence in the single largest Protestant sect in the United States. It has only been a few years since Jesse Helms, an Über-Baptist, called for a government-sanctioned internment of AIDS patients.

My fear of an American incarnation of the Holocaust for gay people may seem extreme. I recall that the majority of Germans thought the Fascists were comical. They were all quite entertained until the state made it permissible to vent all of their social dissatisfactions on one group of people. I cannot help but doubt that America's Moral Majority is any more moral than the majority of Germans in the 1930s.

How can I draw such outlandish comparisons? Not only can I read, but I am born and bred of these people. I was immersed in that culture. I watched and listened until I was an early adolescent and began to distance myself from the schizoid break between being a Christian and being a Baptist. The more I began to think for myself, the clearer it became that those two moral contexts were mutually exclusive.

Thinking is the key. Both Joe's and my own disavowal of the Southern Baptist Church had less to do with awareness of being gay in the midst of a brutally dismissive belief system than it did with our own ability to blindly accept the contradictions inherent in Baptist doctrine and practice. Somewhere along the line we stopped believing we were innately sinful and evil.

In a personal renaissance, we each embraced the notion that we were actually special and good children of a God who didn't exist merely to set us up to fail. Our daily lives were test enough. Survival as gay children required us to mine a deep sense of uniqueness in the face of unrelenting conformity. We were pedaling as hard as we could to be acceptable to our world. Conceding that even that effort was, at best, doomed and damned was too hopeless.

Intellectually curious, precocious even, we asked questions for which Baptist doctrine had no answers. Fortunately for us, we were born to participate in society's questioning period, which the 1960s defined. Looking for answers to our very existence with our minds as well as the faith drilled into us from infancy brought us to the altar. We came away empty-handed. The answers that were proffered were simplistic and generalized, for the consumption of sheep, not thinkers or queers.

Is there a "gay" viewpoint or a "queer" perspective? Of course, and it doesn't appear at puberty. That way of looking at the world comes viscerally at birth, not through some pink sunglasses put on at whim.

Joe recalls, at eleven, sitting in church over several Sunday mornings with an extremely heightened awareness. He remembers being spoken to directly by God, not in words, but in an immediate cerebral understanding of a simple message. He says he always knew he wouldn't grow up to get married and have children. This was a certainty for him even before he had an awareness of the mechanics of sex roles or sexual attraction.

Comprehending this truth about himself, Joe remembers God calling him to be a missionary. Anyone familiar with the Southern Baptist Church knows of its historical preoccupation with missionary ministry. We had the Lottie Moon Christmas Offering to help Baptist Missions in China; we had Home Missions; we had mission fields in every conceivable place on earth. Knowing this, it might be easy to dismiss Joe's direct communication from God as the overheated imaginings of an impressionable child. That dismissal is unfair.

Joe further explains that this persistent call to missionary work was directly linked in his consciousness to his understanding that he would never marry. He wanted to serve. He wanted to take part in a meaningful way in God's work. Aware of his aberrant future within the context of his world, he didn't want his faith or his role to be marginalized. As it was common, if unspoken, knowledge that nice, Christian Southern ladies couldn't be sent out among the wanton heathens, the mission field seemed the perfect place for young Joe to take his obvious otherness to perform God's will.

Imagine this precocious little boy trying as hard as he could to find a place for himself within the context of social and religious service. Excruciatingly self-aware of the reality of his existence as "other," he responded to the call in the best way he could.

Those unfamiliar with Southern Baptist religious services wouldn't know of the "altar call." At the conclusion of each sermon, simultaneous with the lugubrious closing hymn, the pastor descends from the pulpit to stand in front of the congregation to receive sinners and saved alike who wish to make a public profession of faith or to rededicate their lives to God. This public and highly emotional display in front of the entire congregation of the faithful is the only way to be "saved."

For three straight Sundays, Joe made his way down the aisle to whisper his confession that the Lord was calling him. His mother, of course, was beside herself. Aisle walking was a very public confession of something deeply disturbing. What on earth could be going on in her little boy's life that would necessitate such a continuous need to address the pastor? Worse, what in heaven's name must the rest of the church be thinking? What must be going on in the Riddick family to bring their middle son so often to the altar?

Joe kept his own counsel. In the complex but clear meditations on his one-way communication with God, there was much he knew he couldn't share; too much in that call related directly to his most private self.

His mother gave up asking him and went to the pastor. He readily told her of Joe's assertion that the Lord was calling him as a missionary. The pastor blithely disregarded Joe's privacy to ease his mother's anxiety at her family's public embarrassment.

Joe has never recovered from this violation of his confidence. It is easy to dismiss the musings of a child. For a variety of practical reasons, a child's sophisticated claims of a personal revelation from God might be dismissed as fantasy or, worse, as a mere precocious mirroring of larger concepts. The damning result of either conceit is the humiliation of the child's perceptions in regard to his or her intent, intelligence, and faith.

Joe's personal call from God has manifested itself in some very real ways, despite its earlier belittlement. His mother appropriated his desire to become a missionary for herself and, indeed, accomplished it in fact. Joe has assumed an equally great secular mission ministry in a variety of ways. He was among the first voices in Tidewater Virginia to promote AIDS awareness and education. He has spent a large part of his professional life in the past thirteen years in the provision of AIDS-related services.

Once, I called Joe at work to rattle on about a trivial personal trauma. After I wound down, I asked what was up with him. After a long pause, he replied simply that he was just staring at his desk, not getting much done. After a little prodding, he explained that his desktop held five urns containing the ashes of people he had known. The urns were all that was left of clients, acquaintances, even friends. Abandoned by their families, it was up to Joe to decide what to do with them.

I wonder sometimes at the depth of that kind of commitment to peripheral people. I am rarely altruistic or very aware of others. But then, I never had a call from God. I will not dismiss the veracity of his memory of God speaking to him. I cannot explain the scope of his commitment to others any other way.

I cannot claim to have heard God's voice, but I did respond to the "altar call" to salvation at a very young age. Each and every Sunday, I heard that the only way to avoid hell was to accept Christ as your personal savior. As life was portrayed in church as being brief and brutal, it was a tried-and-true technique for the pastor to ask his congregation, rhetorically, "What would you do if you met the Lord on the way home?"

The inference was simple. If you got killed in a car accident on the way home, would you be going to heaven or hell? The answer was as blunt as the question. If you weren't "saved," you'd be heading straight for hell. I quickly figured it out and walked my little six-year-old butt down the aisle and made my profession of faith.

Despite the fact that the concept was simple enough for any six-year-old to comprehend, my early profession of faith caused some consternation among the faithful. Many doubted that I grasped the depth of the commitment. I certainly knew the depth of hell; I'd been told about it for as long as I could remember. After some questioning from the pastor, I was found to be in full possession of the concept and was duly baptized and accepted into the congregation as a full church member.

Professing a faith is easy enough. Developing a daily dialogue with God is far more difficult. If being a Christian were only an exercise in following a script, it would be simple. Nothing worth having ever comes that easily. There are diversions of the mind and of the flesh. The very real nature of the world demands ruthlessness and treachery. Reconciling a persona built for survival with turning the other cheek is damned tough business. Looking back now, I realize I was ready to begin that work—yes, at six.

I emerged glistening in my white shirt and black slacks from a baptism of total immersion. Baptists are tough. You have to go all the way under to be cleansed of your sins. Yet, the stain of original sin is impossible to get out, according to the Baptists. Like the ghost of spilled wine (or Welch's grape juice), it lingers for your whole life to remind you where you came from. Dripping, I made my way out of the baptismal pool and into the world of the born again. I had a lot to get used to.

The first thing I found difficult wasn't ignoring the call of the bottle or the bong. The first thing I had to adjust to was having no gray areas in my sight. In the world of the born-again Christian, there is no gray, only black and white, right and wrong. In the years of my life as a Baptist prior to puberty, I became aware that to be right, I had to do right. Sadly, the only way to do right was to surrender my mind.

Most born-again Christians have the same addictive personalities that led them to disaster prior to the altar. An addictive personality recognizes no reality other than the need. It's only a short twelve steps from the clinic to the arms of the Baptists or any other similar Protestant sect. If you surrender your mind, the need will go away. All will be well.

Along with that, you have to surrender a larger sense of social justice, and even rationality. Faith, I was told, had nothing to do with the intellect. Either you believed or you didn't; it was that cut and dried. Even as a child, I couldn't give up my gray areas. Gay even then, I was always aware that my entire existence was a gray area. I surely couldn't color inside so many tightly drawn lines. Early on I began to separate my relationship with God from his church.

With youthful arrogance, I came to dismiss the Baptists as a group of well-meaning idiots who had an immense need to reinforce one another's delusions. They did little in their actions to dissuade me of my convictions.

Joe recalls abandoning his Wednesday night youth group to attend the Presbyterian one across town with his friends. His Baptist youth group leader was incensed. She called him at home to tell him he was "ordered" to stop attending the Presbyterian youth group. She curtly reminded him he was a Baptist youth, not a Presbyterian one. He did not belong there. Joe resented being told where he belonged or didn't, and he told her so. He never went back to Baptist youth service. Indeed, his days as a Baptist were becoming numbered. So were mine, but for somewhat different reasons.

I don't recall what led me to Nietzsche. With a hungry, if undisciplined, mind, my claims to individuality were fierce. To be a queer kid is to be assaulted daily by every nuance of conformity. Rebellion against that conformity can take some bizarre forms. I read. Seeing myself as under siege by a variety of institutions bent on making me into something I wasn't, Nietzsche's concept of superman, a superior human being, not bound by generally accepted concepts of right and wrong, appealed to me mightily. For my fourteen-year-old self, depressed sometimes to the point of inertia, every day was a triumph of the will.

My parents, witnesses to the outward displays of my inner darkness, were not happy with my choice of reading material. Although knowing they could do little to cure my mental health, they believed they could do plenty to save my spiritual health.

I recall the pastor at the time, a doctor of theology no less, being called on to discuss my mental infatuation with Nietzsche. After my unsatisfying (to him) deconstruction of Kierkegaard, he suggested I turn to the classics.

I felt as if I was being told to read Sally, Dick, and Jane after the rigors of the old German's prose. Finishing *Ecce Homo* and having exhausted my local book sources for further Nietzsche, I remembered my pastor's advice to read the classics. More to get my parents off my back than anything else, I read Plato. After *Symposium,* I remained open to anything having to do with ancient Greece.

With my testosterone levels canceling out my serotonin problems, philosophy rapidly gave way to trashy historical fiction. I discovered Frank Yerby novels and self-abuse at exactly the same time. In a roundabout way, I was introduced to *Phaedo* by a graduate of Southern Baptist Theological Seminary. In an earnest attempt to move away from the dangers of existentialism, my pastor helped me find my way to Greek notions of eros. The Lord works in mysterious ways.

Not so mysterious, it seems all roads lead to Rome. For Joe and me, the contradictions and personal intrusiveness of our Baptist upbringings pushed us from our pews and on toward the eternal city. Searching for a religion less rawboned and emotional, more intellectual and politely distant, Joe began attending High Church Episcopal masses in college. I began my path toward Roman Catholicism in high school.

It seems a contradiction in terms. Why go from the frying pan into the fire? What led us so far from the simple, spartan churches of our pasts? In a sense, wasn't our conversion simply exchanging one dogma of repression and hypocrisy for another? What was so earth-shattering about exchanging straitjackets?

I have asked that question myself. I have asked Joe. The answers are varied and come to no single conclusion. The whole effort of trying to explain a choice of faith is to walk a tightrope over deep canyons of emotionalism or tail-chasing philosophy. The choice of a faith to practice is based on a visceral attraction, not a cerebral one. In any event, the diverse answers only illuminate the continuing path of spirituality in both our lives.

Joe was first drawn to the Episcopal Church by its music. As a music major in college, he was required to participate in a choral group. Of course, as with all art, the church was a powerful and persistent patron. Many great wonders of classical music were crafted for the church. Joe went. Joe sang. Joe became enticed by the richness of the experience.

Joe says that he was drawn not only by the music but by the beauty of the liturgy. Although great passion and release may be found in the delivery of a Baptist sermon, there is very little beauty. The simple service of the original Protestants has evolved into a crude bludgeoning in Baptist practice. Virulently antipopish and anti-intellectual, the liturgy of the Baptist church is at best unsubtle, if not bordering on illiterate.

Both Joe and I were accustomed to that type of church service. Being grabbed by the spiritual throat and shaken allows little opportunity for transcendence. Imagine the joy in being seduced into a dialogue with God through beauty. The mark of a successful Baptist sermon was my mother saying, "He sure stepped on some toes today." Mass, with its focused language of call and response, was an offering of simple solace and instruction to a soul already whipped by the world.

Joe loved the smells and bells of the High Church Anglo-Catholic service. He loved the dignified progression of the priest and acolytes behind the crucifix. He felt his spirits lifted by the hymnody. The theater and drama served to transport him from the mundane world into a reverent place, not of the world, but of the promise of heaven to come. God in that church was approached with dignity and decorum, not with sullen cowering.

I fell in love with that part of it as well. And for one who prided himself on his individuality, I did, and do, appreciate the Roman Catholic Church for placing me in communion with a diverse and worldwide population. There is a sense of awe in being a part of a history, bloody and flawed though it may be, that extends back directly to Christ.

That is the intellectual answer to the question of my choice of religion. Mass is lovely. The liturgy is concise and thoughtful. The feeling of continuity is pleasing as well. The visceral reason, however, is more personal and less complex.

Part of the Roman Catholic Mass involves the communicant kneeling after the consecration of the Host. The communicant says, "Lord, I am not worthy to receive you, but only say the word and I shall be healed." Before I was a catechumen, I said those words along with everyone else. I said them and I waited. How do I describe the many things that made me feel so wrong, so bad, so unworthy? I had been taught by the Baptist Church that we are conceived in sin, live in sin, and will struggle unsuccessfully against that sinful nature all of our lives. Compounded by that, I was a pretty kid in a world that made constant torture of pretty boys a team sport. Worse, I really was queer. Isolated by accident of birth beyond the common conception in sin, I felt absolutely alone and hurting all the time.

In my waiting, I felt an odd sense of warmth expand in my chest. I felt forgiveness, but, even more, I felt complete and total understanding, acceptance, and love. I had not found that anywhere else, although I had been looking for a long time. I looked for it in the eyes of every lover and friend. I looked for it in mental health clinics. I looked for it in carefully measured bong hits and thin razor-crafted lines of toot. That feeling was only visceral and real in one place. Church. Catholic Church.

Joe and I extended our infatuation with our chosen religious practices to the point of formal conversion. Joe was in a pew at Holy Redeemer by the Sea when I took my first Holy Communion. Although converting at different points in our lives we shared that experience just as we had coming out as gay men. In a perverse parallel, religious conversion is a mirror experience of coming out.

Without inviting a tedious and pointless discussion of the "conversion" of straight men to homosexuality, or "conversion" of homosexuals to straight, born-again Christians, I draw the parallel differently. A lot of blood has been shed, a lot of pain has been caused, in the pursuit of religious identity. Traditions are acquired through sacrifice and pain. The freedom to express religious beliefs has caused mass migrations and scarred the collective psyche of humankind.

During one year, I acknowledged my previously undiscussed sexuality to my parents and, later, announced I had converted to Roman Catholicism. My mother was aghast that I would deny centuries of Puritan forebears to become Roman Catholic. I think she'd always known I was queer; Catholic came as a complete surprise.

My mother was either so battered by my earlier confession or so uncomfortable with my change of religious affiliation that she folded her arms across her bosom and said, commandingly, "That's it. You can't do anything else for ten years. My heart can't stand any more."

In one tumultuous year, I had turned my back on everything that she had worked for years to ensure. She believed she had handed me a future in relatively good order. Essentially, I was saying thanks, but no thanks, which earned me the terse declaration, "I gave birth to you. Everything after that is your doing."

Not entirely. Although I have spent a lifetime obstinately defending an ever-expanding sense of self, I cannot claim complete self-creation. Always, that inner directive, the inner communication with the divine, keeps me surefooted on the tightrope. Perhaps I am more Baptist than Catholic when I claim faith because, at some point, I did surrender a part of my mind. I had to. You don't willfully turn your back on everything just to be yourself. If you re-create yourself, you have the responsibility of doing right, even if you look like you're doing it all wrong.

In Joe's High Church Episcopal world, there is a politically debated, but clear, tolerance of gay people. The doctors of dogma may argue the point, but in simple practice, Episcopalians are a relatively tolerant bunch. So much so that Joe and his partner, Brad, enjoyed the blessings of their church in a union ceremony.

Joe's mother cried. She cajoled. She pouted. But she came. With her aplomb wrapped tastefully about her, she gave her approval by her presence. Mothers evolve along with the world. Traditions retain their validity, even when they are adapted and conversions are made.

I have found such adaptations and conversions made to the simplest traditions and social expectations in my own life. Less than a year following Joe and Brad's union cermony found me settling into a partnership with a wonderful man named Jeff. Like me, Jeff is Roman Catholic. Once we began living together, I started attending Mass at his church, ultimately becoming a member of the parish. Along with my membership came some social obligations on my part and some small adaptation on the church's. The validity of some traditions managed to be upheld on both our parts.

When our parish church began building a school, they solicited the parishioners for pledges over the phone. Jeff's name comes far earlier in the alphabet than mine, so they got to him first. As he is a cradle Catholic, the church's constant fund-raising and school's needs are part and parcel of his life. (His father had even worked bingo on Friday nights to help offset his and his brother's parochial school tuition.) Jeff was reconciled, even pleased, at the prospect of making a pledge to support the school's construction. To me, it was no big deal. We slated determination of our pledge amount for a budget discussion that was constantly postponed. When the phone solicitor called him, he artfully stalled the commitment. After a couple of weeks, the solicitors made it to the "Q's."

A pleasant woman gave me the pitch, to which I replied that my family had not yet determined how much we could contribute. She responded that she had me listed as a single person. Ever the artful dodger, I told her I was part of a nontraditional household. Persistent, she explained that she could lump "all of youse" under a single-offering envelope. All I had to do was give her the envelope number.

Obligingly, I gave her Jeff's number. I heard the clicking of the computer keys and tried to imagine her response when the database matched a name to the number. There was a brief period of silence. She said, questioningly, that she had that number as belonging to a Jeffrey A. . . . I told her that was correct.

After a brief silence, I heard the computer keys clicking away. I imagined our envelope number speeding along a hotline to the Vatican. There, this same number would trigger a same-sex alarm, causing us both to be excommunicated. At last, she said, "Congratulations. In the eyes of the bookkeeping department of this church, you two guys are a family."

Though I believed I was long past needing even the bookkeeping department's acknowledgment of my union, I felt warmed by the inclusion. While I may never walk down the aisle and be married with a full nuptial mass, my commitment to Jeff had been acknowledged and formalized by my church. When the new offering envelope arrived a week later, imprinted with both our names, in an odd combination of hyphens and slashes, I was quietly happy and amused.

Earlier, I said that one must forgive one's parents to make them one's friends. It's no different with the church, Catholic or Baptist. Without disrespect for any individuals who have been harmed by their church, physically or psychically, I think the church requires gay forgiveness on a collective and individual level.

I held a grudge against the Catholic Church for many years. Long before I met Jeff and, with him, returned to regular attendance at Mass, an incident occurred that left me rather angry and distanced me from a critical aspect of the exercise of the faith. During those years, I specifically avoided participating in confession, or, as it's also known, the rite of reconciliation. Reconcilitation requires forgiveness, which, in this case, needed to come from me.

Twelve years ago, I experienced a spontaneous collapsed lung while swimming laps. At the time, I thought it was just a bad cramp so I put off going to the doctor, until my chest became so filled with air that my other lung collapsed. I was placed on a chest pump for a week's stay in the hospital. In the intake paperwork, I listed my religion as Catholic.

On Saturday night, during that hospital stay, a rather officious priest showed up in my room to hear my confession and give me communion. It had been a couple of years since my last confession, and that son of a bitch pulled a chair up to my bed and made me list specific sex acts and how many times I'd performed them in the two years.

I couldn't go anywhere. I was hooked up to a machine. This priest from hell wanted all the gory details, I assume, to fuel later masturbatory fantasies. When he finally had extracted the last detail from me, he gave me absolution and communion. He left with a mouth twisted by distaste and eyes glinting with lust, which combined to create a bizarre mask of unctuous piety. I swore I would never go to confession again.

I didn't, until Holy Week of 1999. I made it through Lent without cheating on abstaining from meat on Fridays, but my self-imposed fast from a couple of other things was less successful. Always a cafeteria Catholic, I had managed to pick and choose among the rituals that satisfied me and ignored those which didn't.

In any event, I decided that I was a bit of a cheat. Holy Week, after all, does hold a great deal of meaning for Christians. When I looked at the balance sheet in my life between sacrifice and self-indulgence, selfishness tipped the scale away from any meaningful emulation of Christ's suffering and death.

Working on the manuscript of this book at the time, I realized that for all my high-flown pronouncements, my commitment to the ideas I was discussing involved more posturing than practice. I had a lot of airy concepts about Catholicism, without the responsibility of the form. I decided to go to a communal penance service on Monday night of Holy Week.

Sometime during the ritual, I decided to make my confession. I had taken such a strong stand on forgiveness in this book, and I had some forgiving myself to do. Just then, I knew if I didn't, I would have felt more the poseur than I already did.

I joined the line for confession with Father Tony. In my large middle-class parish, Father Tony is the main priest. Irish as Patty's pig, he is a masterful pastor to each of the three thousand parishioners of his flock. He is so personable that you feel as if he knows and recognizes you individually in the throng. Our other priest, who is less outgoing, had wisely placed himself in the confessional with the privacy grill. Still, I waited with sweaty palms for my turn in the cry room that was serving as Father Tony's confessional.

Once alone with Father Tony, I nervously took my seat. The formal words prefacing confession escaped me. I said, "Forgive me, Father, I am rusty at this. It's been twelve years since my last confession." Without hesitation, Father Tony responded, with a slight smile, "Relax, it's not brain surgery."

I tried to articulate my sins in a simple summation. Staring at the floor, I admitted I had done many things that I wasn't particularly proud of, but for which I was genuinely sorry. Stumbling pathetically, I explained that I had been trying for several years to become more diligent in the practice of my faith. Afraid of his response, I looked up at the priest sitting across from me.

With an eloquent, dismissive wave, Father Tony said, "Don't be so hard on yourself." Awkwardly, yet appropriately, I said, "Thank you, Father." After giving me a slight, but meaningful, penance, Father Tony granted me absolution and gave me a blessing. Grateful and aware that many were waiting after me, I started to stand.

Father Tony surprised me by motioning for me to stay. To my great surprise, he said, "Tell me, is this church meeting your needs?" I stumbled over myself telling him how much it did. I told him that Jeff and I drove past another Catholic church not five minutes from our house to continue coming to this one after we moved.

The priest nodded, a self-deprecating smile on his face. He said, "I know that I'm good on the altar, but the church has grown so large that I'm afraid that I have lost personal touch with many of my parishioners." Anxious to reassure him, I reminded Father Tony of his attendance on a former neighbor of mine as he lay dying a number of years ago.

This neighbor was a lapsed Catholic whose wife was Russian Orthodox. Dying, he asked for last rites. Father Tony obliged him and even conducted his funeral mass in the chapel of our church during Holy Week that year. Father Tony recalled the man's name without prompting.

"I know you have a lot of people pulling on you," I said. "But you don't know how much I admired you for being there for my neighbor, even though he wasn't a parishioner." It was true. That was only one instance of this priest's compassion that I knew of personally. Father Tony thanked me and, shaking my hand, asked me to remember him in my prayers.

I went to the altar and did my penance. Leaving the church, I felt curiously light, and confused as well. I had expected to be chastised. I had expected to be reminded of my willful sins and my unworthiness of salvation. Instead, I received empathy from a man who had some of the same doubts about the practice of his spiritual commitment that I did.

Absolution, it seems, is a two-way street. So is reconciliation. The essence of spiritual commitment lies in the ongoing dialogue between each individual and the divine. The anger in words at a church, Baptist or Catholic or whatever, is still a dialogue. For me, religion requires a conversation. For Joe, right now, religion is a confrontation. For either of us, the communication persists with the need of long association.

At the beginning of preparation for this book, I asked Joe where he was with the whole religion deal. From an upbringing that fostered enough homophobia to lead his parents to consider aversion therapy as a cure for his sexual identity, to a union ceremony in an environment that has helped to sustain an eleven-year relationship, Joe has run the spiritual gamut. He continues to go to church sporadically. But after all these years, he has come to a schism between religiosity and spirituality.

Joe's questioning is less emotional than intellectual; it is born of simple spiritual erosion. The little boy who heard God call him to be a missionary has spent too many years staring at too many funeral urns. The vast moral obligation he felt to help in saving even a few from the AIDS plague has brought him more questions than answers.

The beauty and allure of faith for Joe have always lain in the hymns and liturgy of his chosen church. Unfortunately, there is little dignity and beauty in disease and early death. The call of God is muted and made obtuse by the harsh requirements of doing that very thing he was called by God to do. Past the lovely music and pretty words of praise, Joe has very real questions regarding religion's inept role in such elemental issues as social justice.

Nearing the completion of this book, I received an e-mail from Joe stating that he and Brad had visited their old parish church in Portsmouth after a few years' absence. They were welcomed back warmly. For many years, Joe sang in the choir, composed liturgy, and was a lector. He was told that his choir robe and vestments were waiting for him, hanging still where he had left them.

He tentatively said he wanted to start going back. There is, after all, a spiritual hunger and sense of home that church feeds and fulfills. Even in the face of great intellectual conflict and disillusionment, the church remains. Bigger than our definitions of it, beyond our questioning, the church requires you to make your own peace with it.

Joe and I disagree on the methods to make that peace. We even disagree on what church is all about. For Joe, church is about community. For me, community is only a small part of it. In my point of view, church is about paying formal respect to God. I will admit to an abstruse presentation of my personal beliefs. Only in attempting to articulate them do I find that my reasoning is convoluted and often contradictory. But in the effort lies my authentic, if flawed, perspective.

In my thinking, God has very little to do with any version of his church. If you look at the entire history of blood, hypocrisy, and hatred in the Catholic, Episcopal, or Baptist Churches, specifically, you note a pronounced lack of Christianity. "Church" is really a locus for the public expression of personal faith. As such, it is a microcosm of the world as a whole. With the reconciliation of a gay identity with being a part of a larger world comes the impetus to change that world. So it is with the church.

Many people, gay and straight, feel there is no place at the table for them in the church of their upbringing, and there is a great sense of loss in their alienation. So much of the ordering of our lives comes from relating events that define it by seasons and symbols.

I find great peace in watching the passing of the liturgical year. My life is ordered by the transition from ordinary time to Lent to Advent. St. Francis's Feast Day and my parish's blessing of the animals are heralds of the approaching holidays. I drag my two brute dogs to church for their blessing and note the position of the sun in the western sky. The days grow shorter. The sun reaches toward its year-end solstice.

That my church, on a very public level, condemns and persecutes a part of my identity is difficult and demeaning. While my anger at that fact will never take me to Saint Patrick's Cathedral to desecrate the host, I try to express resistance through my constant presence. One needn't scream to get the point across. I make no attempt to conceal my identity to my church. My protest is my refusal to abandon the church. Unreformed and uncompromising, I insert myself into the life of my parish.

Intellectually, my resistance comes in applying the church's view of me back onto the church itself. It is bad theology, but it is the stated position of the church to hate the sin, but love the sinner. That spiritual sleight of hand works for me as well. My church is very good with mental gymnastics. I became good at them too.

With its glacial canonical speed, the Roman Catholic Church now says it's not so terrible to be gay, but it is terrible to have sex outside of marriage. Since the Church will not marry gay people, they must live in sin. However, everyone lives in sin. Everyone is also pardoned from sin by confession. In this, the mental gymnastics the Church requires of gay people are no different from those required of straight people. As with much else, the rhetoric of religion is all semantics.

The Church is worse than the IRS in setting you up to fail and then giving you a loophole to circumvent its displeasure. Likewise, I give the Church every chance to rethink its laws, although I have no fundamental respect for those laws at all. In my opinion and practice, if you are square with God, then you are above the Church's petty and pernicious legal quibbling. If you sincerely attempt to create a meaningful dialogue with the divine, Church law is immaterial.

Joe does not understand how I can partition my conscience this way. Far better read in the area of liberation theology than I am, he thinks my attitude is an abrogation of my responsibility to the larger gay community. My response is, yes, the Church, my church, any church is culpable for the spiritual and physical violence it continues to condone against gay people.

In that regard, the Church is indefensible. But, you cannot effect change from outside an institution. Neither can you adequately assess its distortion and ineffectiveness from a blind position within it. For me, there must be a simultaneity of being at once in the Church, but not of the Church. The one perspective for me is from the vantage point of being above the law. Without an ongoing dialogue with the divine, that is impossible.

No one rides for free. No one gets a break when it comes to religion. Everyone has issues. The root source of the issues, however, has little to do with the Church and much to do with the individual's personal relationship with the divine. Issues with the

Church become a convenient rationalization to avoid confrontation with the spiritual aspect of one's life. It is so much easier to attempt to change the world than to change the Church. But that effort is all of one piece. The more meaningful effort is in creating an individual relationship with God.

I have been a Catholic now longer than I was a practicing Baptist. I don't give a good goddamn for those who think I am only an accommodating assimilationist. Or, that I am simply a suburban, heterosexual manqué. I am not individually responsible for the salvation of the Church, the gay community, or the world.

I am responsible for my salvation. I sincerely believe if my efforts are genuine, then my tiny part of the whole will effect change or growth in the larger social, sexual, and religious communities of which I am a part. Many voices shouting creates the incomprehensible dialectic of the mob. A single voice, speaking in anger or reconciliation, can make a point be heard. I believe responsibility lies in making that individual point.

The fundamental part of my personal faith comes from a sense of responsibility, first to God, then to myself, and in the exercise of that responsibility, the needs of the world will be serviced. Ultimately, I believe I will answer to God only for myself.

I cannot adhere soley to the rhetoric of the gay community, the Democratic Party, or Wall Street. Each becomes its own religion instead of only parts of the whole of my world. The Roman Catholic Church doesn't dictate my spirituality any more than the polemics of the secular religions of liberation, politics, or economics do. My religion, as seemingly self-centered as it may be, works for me, or rather my spirituality has grown around that religion like wisteria climbs a tree.

Joe has always disagreed with my overwhelming sense of singularity. It is out of character for me to care much for anyone's opinion. Still, Joe is the only person in this world to whom I would attempt to justify my spirituality. Joe is my social and gay conscience. In that, I have put him in the uncomfortable position of being confessor and representative of all gay people. However, without his direct challenge to my theological pretensions, they would remain only that. As with much else, Joe's position of mentor includes providing the intellectual whetstone that sharpens pretension to conviction.

Chapter 5

Mind Games

I have read that the sense of smell is the most powerful memory inducer. It takes little more than a whiff of white paste or freshly sharpened pencils to evoke the memory of school. Those are the pleasant recollections of education. The reality of the educational experience is somewhat different.

For the gifted child, education prior to college is really an exercise in discipline as much as instruction. Both gifted children, Joe and I were disciplined and instructed in public school settings. Our consensus of opinion is that our precollege education was unremarkable in the extreme. Our early schooling really only provided a mise-en-scène for the true experience of education. We learned to teach ourselves about what we loved on our own. The most meaningful education of that time came primarily through outside reading.

If you look at the weighted shelves in either of our homes, you can see the evidence of a lifelong love affair with books. I spent far more on books than I ever spent on clothes. Joe is better dressed, but his bookshelves provide an entire history of a mind that is as well put together as his impeccably dressed form.

The greatest accomplishment of our youthful education was to instill and encourage in us a love of reading. That this accomplishment came out of the overall poverty of the education itself says all that can be said about the public schools of the South in the 1960s and 1970s.

Our best education, and most influential, came outside of the schoolhouse. That education was a lonely apprenticeship in learning the craft and techniques of what we loved most. For me, it was an exuberant, untutored development of an innate ability to draw and paint. For Joe, it was music. For both of us, it was the first rebellion against conformity and a testing ground of the strengths we would use in later assertions of our gay identities.

Joe recalls being given piano lessons by an older bachelor teacher. The lessons themselves were rigorous and thoroughly proper, but with the pull to music came the first exposure to others with gay identities.

Joe's piano teacher was one of the stereotypical men of the South who were a little funny, but awfully good to their mamas. In the relative tolerance at the end of this century, it is unkind to make any revisionist suppositions about the deprived kind of life embraced by the piano teacher, but the reward for living such a life was the scores of children who learned music from him.

Following graduation from college with a degree in music education, Joe returned to visit this teacher. A surge of gratitude often comes with the awarding of a degree in anything, in addition to that pride which demands acknowledgment of the master from the former apprentice. Joe told his childhood instructor all about his accomplishments and his earnest plans for a career in music. The piano teacher, grown elderly and irascible, told him, "Well, I see you've become a homo."

Joe laughs about it now. He says he thought the old man said he'd become a "hobo," but the piano teacher bluntly corrected him. There are two ways of looking at the piano teacher's rude pronouncement. One might be to view it as envy of his former pupil's youth and apparent freedom; the other, as the reactionary bitterness of a life spent in self-surveillance and frustration.

Whatever. The lesson was learned, the debt acknowledged, and the gratitude proffered. The results of Joe's piano lessons, the tedious scales and tormented recitals, had blossomed into a special facet of his identity that continues to sustain him to this day.

I had no outside art instruction. Throughout elementary school, we had an art teacher who came one morning each month. Even after all these years, I can become invigorated and happy recalling the smooth smear and smell of thick tempera paint or the waxy slide of a Crayola crayon.

Once a month, over five years, I progressed from rolling modeling clay into snakes to a rather ambitious 24″ × 36″ mosaic of the

Madonna and Child made from hundreds of carefully cut one-eighth-inch squares of construction paper. That effort earned exhibition in a local bank's Christmas display. I still remember the excitement of seeing it hung in the bank's lobby.

My artistic ambitions weren't limited to school. I had sketchbooks. I painted watercolors. I bought small pieces of pre-gessoed canvas stretched over cardboard and painted tiny images of people, heavily inspired by Modigliani. One of these hung over my grandmama's kitchen door as long as she lived.

Encouraged by the approval from my grandmama and my parents, I painted and drew with great openness and enthusiasm until I reached fifth grade. Nearing the end of my tenure in elementary school, I thought about how much I had enjoyed the instruction of Mrs. Thompson, the art teacher, over the years. I decided to make her a picture.

In an effort to teach us something about art history, Mrs. Thompson had spent most of the year showing us great paintings by placing a copy of Janson's or Gardiner's *History of Art* on an opaque projector and shining their color prints onto the roll-up filmstrip screen. I fell in love with the scope and grandeur of the large historical panoramas.

Choosing the burning of Joan of Arc as my theme, I spent hours drawing a detailed pen-and-ink piece as a thank-you parting gift for all the joy in art Mrs. Thompson had given me. By the end of fifth grade, I had been under outpatient treatment at the local mental health clinic for several months. Due to a rather bitchy note left in my permanent record by a teacher, I was a bit of a scandal at Virginia Street School. Of course, at the time, I didn't know that I scared the hell out of them.

I can laugh now at the look I imagine crossed poor Mrs. Thompson's face when she plucked out my detailed drawing of the execution of Joan of Arc, along with my well-penned note expressing my gratitude for her art instruction. No wonder the poor woman avoided me like the plague the rest of the year.

Then, I only felt a terrible hurt and an overwhelming sense of failure. I had worked hard on that epic drawing. I just wanted Mrs. Thompson to understand that she had taught me a way of seeing and a way of sharing. For that, I remain grateful, despite the fact that her rejection hurt at the time. Mrs. Thompson taught me more than a love for creating art. She also inflicted the first rough abrasion on a tender skin that had to toughen into a thick hide if I was going to be an artist. After that, I continued to draw and paint, but I wasn't so ready to share.

For me, Mrs. Thompson was followed by Mrs. Rouse and then Mr. Blount, as I continued taking all the art classes available to me in public school. Joe continued his pedestrian lessons with the closeted piano teacher. Following our emancipation from public school, we both had the opportunity to continue our artistic instruction in college.

Our identities as artists informed our nascent identities as gay men. It is an absorbing task to pull ideas from your brain and express them through your fingers. That absorption creates an exquisite sense of self that excludes the world at large. It tends the growth of a complex interior landscape that is often far more real and rich than the one outside the mind. That interior landscape becomes a place of strength from which to observe and interpret the straight world.

Creative efforts demand a clear sense of self in the realm of the abstract. That self is strengthened formidably, and the resulting interior life achieves a discipline and set of values that is almost entirely inner directed. With no external direction in the formulation of a gay identity, inner direction is essential to forming a strong sense of self.

Inner-directed children are a nightmare in a system that is geared for the training of sheep. Each child's sense of individuality demands a fundamental resistance to any attempts to thwart or direct individual growth. However, human beings are herd animals. Educational systems are based on the assumption that children are outer directed. For the creative child, inner directives cause behavior that is often called rebellious or antisocial, when it is essentially only a fierce desire to maintain a vastly stronger interior life. As a gay identity is also considered "antisocial," the desire to follow inner directives is reinforced by the creative drive, forming an amazingly resilient ego.

Psychoanalytic ego theory debates from Freud through Lacan have centered on the notion that ego strength is determined by both biological maturation and successful socialization. For the creative or gay child, the instinctual sense of self-preservation is stronger than the instinct for successful socialization. Educational systems act as a sort of in loco parentis for the collective ego that neutralizes and regulates the more instinctual individual id in the continuing process of individual adaptation.

Beyond such clinical musings, psychoanalytic theory is baffled by the development of the creative individual. From Freud's reverent psychoanalytic deconstruction of Leonardo da Vinci to Lacan's observation on Baroque statuary as evocative of his concept of *jouissance,* creative individuals and their products intrigue and captivate. Still, psychoanalytic fascination with the creative individual has come to no collective opinion regarding creativity's source or survival. Theory fails in the reality of practice. The resilience of creative adaptation is amazing.

Physiological and environmental determinants are at once simple and complex. Being left-handed, I was smacked on the back of the hand with a ruler every time my first grade teacher caught me holding my pencil in my left hand. Finally, my mother noticed my bruised knuckles and called the teacher. My mother told her to stop trying to force me into right-handedness. As an infant, my parents tried to break me of my left-handedness by refusing to give me my bottle until I took it with my right hand. I would take the bottle with my right hand and promptly put it in my left to nurse.

In a lifetime of left-handedness, my poor body has experienced many broken bones, cuts, and other injuries resulting from that split-second's time necessary to adapt to a world oriented to right-handed people. In a natural extension, my mind has been thwarted by the time it takes to adapt to linear thinking modes. Beyond that, there is the psychic damage of adapting a clear sense of sexual identity to the compelling sexual norms of this time and culture. Yet, the tenacity of the effort is testament to the elemental nature of the inclination.

If you look at educational systems as a form of socialization and adaptation for the individual, you begin to notice their emphasis on conformity and collectivization of experience. Socially, the hegemony of those quick to respond to this normalization over the more individualistic creative or queer personalities actually becomes the tempering through fire for the creative or queer spirit.

I cannot imagine any occupation lower on the desirability scale for Southern, white, middle-class parents of the 1960s and 1970s than that of a musician or an artist. Giftedness in those areas may provoke a certain closeted sense of parental pride, but they were hardly socially acceptable gifts to be publicly celebrated.

For the socially ambitious middle class of that time and place, it was a joyful obligation to expose one's children to cultural opportunities unavailable to the parents when they were young. To be "well-rounded" a child must have an appreciation of the arts. However, a child discovered to have a talent in the arts was the cause of certain consternation. It is one thing to be able to entertain a group of friends gathered around the piano or to be able to draw an appropriately representational rendering of a bowl of fruit. It was quite another to cross the line by becoming a fruitcake artsy type.

After high school, I entered college with the luxury of having already met my freshman liberal arts requirements by taking them in community college while still a high school student. My first year in college, I was able to take mainly art courses. When I announced I was going to transfer to another school with a better art department, my parents' reaction wasn't exactly enthusiastic.

Although I had been overtly artistic for my entire life, they were expecting me to tire of it in college. As with homosexuality, I was coming to a point in my life where they felt I should be outgrowing the artistic ambitions. My father was quick to remind me that I needed to quit "coloring" to learn a salable skill. I finally buckled under pressure. I switched my major to urban planning, the bastard stepchild of political science and architecture. Responsible for my own educational bills after my undergraduate years, I ran to architecture for my master's. Now after all these years, I enjoy reminding my father that I have managed to make a living "coloring" for most of my adult life.

Joe's parents weren't necessarily thrilled with his major in college either. Music hardly seemed an adult occupation. Also, musicians, like artists, were socially suspect and marginalized in the culture of the middle-class South. To our parents, it seemed as if we were "just throwing away" their hard-earned social status (and money).

Joe redeemed himself somewhat by taking the courses necessary to earn teaching certification. Teaching school was a bit de classe, but it was far more socially acceptable than being a mere musician.

After our formal education, both Joe and I continued our commitments to our creative endeavors. Joe eventually segued into interior design as an occupation and elevated community service into a form of theater. Eventually, he briefly took a job as the director for a regional theater company.

While supporting myself, either as a draftsman or an art director, I began to take my painting seriously. I made my way from small, local juried shows to larger regional ones. I moved from Kill Devil Hills to Raleigh, partly to have access to more artistic opportunities. By that time, I was influenced heavily by the technical virtuosity of Philip Pearlstein, with the decidedly pictorial approach of a queer Eric Fischl.

I painted epic canvases of nude males in the company of vicious dogs and the dogs' dying prey. I had some issues. I came home to my dining room/studio one day to find my poor mother and father standing before a $5' \times 6'$ canvas of a nude man with a massive erection sitting next to a pit bull with a bleeding rabbit in its mouth. My roommate had let them in for a visit without putting a sheet over the piece. My mother said, "That's the best dog you've ever painted." My father motioned toward the threateningly impressive penis of the figure and said, "I don't know who you've been hanging out with, but that ain't realism."

I worked for years until I finally got a studio visit from an influential gallery owner in Raleigh, North Carolina. This imposing woman had "made" it. She was respected as an artist in her own right and owned a successful gallery to boot. I served her white wine and changed canvases on the easel for her to peruse while I alternated between bouts of chain-smoking and nervous vomiting off the back porch.

Finally, she nodded at me wearily and said, "You don't know how good you really are. Unfortunately, right now I can do nothing for you." A large amount of her social and financial support rested in the politically conservative, comfortable wealth of the old guard.

They wanted to be challenged by art only to the degree of competitive cocktail conversation. "You won't hang over sofas very well. And politically, Raleigh is too polarized. I am so sorry." Graciously, she told me to keep on working and to keep in touch.

In the woman's defense, that was the time of North Carolina senator Jesse Helms' virulent attack on the National Endowment of the Arts as well as the agencies promoting safe-sex practices through explicitly illustrated pamphlets. No North Carolina gallery dealer in possession of his or her senses wanted to show paintings of menacing homosexuals with threatening dogs.

Disgusted with the political realities of my city, I moved from painting to playing around with video. Eventually, I caught the attention of a local video impresario. This wonderful man was all about dollars and cents, but he loved creative people. With his critical and technical support, I began writing, producing, and directing independent feature-length programming for television.

I was getting some good cable access airtime and a growing reputation as a "serious" talent when I refused to cut the word "fucking" from one of my movies. As a result, that year's worth of work was banned. I had invested so much effort and identified with the project so strongly that it was critical to retain its integrity. I didn't have the resources for a First Amendment fight. Defeated, I took a job as a pool boy/lifeguard and taught little kids swimming lessons for a summer. I moved from North Carolina to South Florida that fall.

Throughout every small success and every large setback, Joe lent his presence and support. When we lived on the beach, he would buy a small piece of art when I was destitute. When I was too poor to afford canvas and stretchers, he helped me cut up $4' \times 8'$ sheets of Masonite to paint on. Once, I finished a piece while I was sick. Joe lent me money to have my prescriptions filled. He took the new piece off my wall, saying, "You owe me money. This piece is mine."

As I became more widely known, Joe traveled to the openings of shows and exhibits in which I was included. He attended the "premiers" of my videos in art galleries and college auditoriums. He suffered through private screenings of the weak early efforts and applauded the technically superior ones. Joe was my critic and my champion.

Just as time will rearrange priorities, so, too, will it rearrange creative endeavors. For many years, Joe channeled all of his creativity toward the fight against AIDS. His music and sense of theater survived for a time in a sort of liturgical half-life as he assumed an active role in his church. Eventually, that, too, was sacrificed to the constant drain of his interior life by the AIDS work.

Occasionally, Joe would call to ask me if he could donate one of the large canvases he was storing for me to be auctioned for fundraising. I'm proud to say my paintings were finally appreciated and bought. The money was no longer important to me; the recognition was riches.

Joe continued his work beyond his burnout. Though immensely experienced, he realized his effectiveness was limited by his lack of formal education credentials. In the world of health care provision, the arrogance of doctors is buttressed and validated by the small set of initials following their names. Again, formal education enters as a defining and qualifying factor in Joe's life.

Joe went back to school. Initially he worked on an MBA within an accelerated program for working professionals. Meeting that obligation, Joe also discovered a hunger for the mental exercise of pursuing an advanced degree. He decided to continue on for his PhD.

Within this advanced context, Joe has discovered that creativity can mutate into theoretical products. As music is merely math one can hear, droning statistics and conflicting modes of management can be made into an individual song to play and sing.

Creativity is a way of looking at reality and the capacity to replicate that perception into a new form to be communicated and consumed. At this writing, Joe is considering for his dissertation a discussion of management issues from a queer theory perspective. As he explained to me in a rush of intellectual excitement, queer theory really grew out of feminist theory and liberation theory. After a year's worth of reading about the applications of those theoretical modes in management techniques, he is seriously looking at the applications of queer theory for management styles.

Joe's role of mentor in my life continues to be defined by his support and intellectual challenge. He brings a vitalizing sense of friendly intellectual competitiveness to my life. From the time that he loaded my arms with gay novels to the time he accepted the slender weight of my own first attempt at fiction, he has remained the most intellectually sympathetic person I have ever met. He, alone, has had the patience to stay with me as my creative endeavors were fueled by manic energy or emotional desolation, all the while maintaining his own intellectual and creative endeavors beyond the Sturm und Drang of mine.

Despite the persistence of bills and the demanding realities of adulthood, Joe and I retain a child's ability to create whole worlds. Creativity forces itself through the concrete of other people's needs and the asphalt of obligation to bear fruit, even if insulted or ignored. Our creative instincts still form a working part of our identities. From piano lessons to grants administration to management theory, or from tempera paint to video cameras to word processors, our mind games expand exponentially with our physical aging.

Chapter 6

Hunters and Gatherers

Gay life, for Joe and me, and for our generation, has been defined by a series of transitions between being sexual hunters or gatherers. We began our sexual lives on a sort of idyllic savanna as gatherers of sensual experience. The search for physical expression of our sexual identities was confined by notions of role-playing and emotional commitment within the familiar boundaries of our youthful experience.

In the real world of gay childhood and adolescence, only chemical scents and telling gestures identify each to the other. But in that time, somehow we begin to know what attracts us and what does not. Sometimes desire occurs before there is a name for it. Even so, the patterns become ingrained and the focus becomes set.

I once had a slightly stupid, but earnest, straight boss ask me when I first knew I was gay. I couldn't really tell him that I had never had a sense of not being gay. Fearful of a stolen glance or two at the occupant of the urinal next to them, many straight men look for some causal explanation for homosexuality. They need to hear a gay man point to a single, specific incident that made him queer so they can inwardly say, "That never happened to me. No way I'm gay."

You can't explain to those guys that there is no queer werewolf whose single violent caress makes you long to hang drapes, style hair, or suck dick. Yet, these straight guys' innocent and transparent earnestness in asking is part and parcel of their appeal. In me, it inspires a sort of weary affection instead of disgust.

Searching for some sort of dumbed-down trope to both reassure and inform this guy, I told him what made me realize I was queer was the 1960s television show *Flipper*. For me, the guys on that

show had this completely perfect existence. They never went to
school. They never had to wear shirts. They had no mother, they got
to swim all the time, *and* they had a dolphin. The clincher was, I
already knew I *really* wanted to go camping with Bud and Sandy
and, especially, their daddy.

The low guttering light that was that boss's intelligence stilled to
a steady flame. He got it, immediately. Looking back now, I can say
that my little example was completely honest and completely apt. I
never could quite figure out if I wanted to be Sandy or to fuck him.
With Sandy's daddy, I had no doubts. If a ten-year-old could come
up with a secret salacious grin, I'm sure I could back then. As a kid,
just thinking of that big, sexy son of a bitch racing along in his boat
behind Flipper to get me out of a jam made me confusingly queasy
and hard.

My entire sexual experience prior to meeting Joe was a quest to
find Sandy or Sandy's daddy. I listened to all of Joe's stories. Pissed
off and hurt by the half-assed version of Sandy's daddy with whom
I was currently living, I began a lifelong comparison and contrast
with Joe's experiences to gauge the authenticity of my own.

The 1970s were a great time to come of age sexually. Both Joe
and I fumbled through our initial sexual experiences with little
difference, except for the six years between their occurrence and
our partners in passion. We had crushes that were unrequited. We
had fantasies that were fulfilled. The real discussion lies in the
avenues that were open to us and our generation at the end of
adolescence.

The ripples of Stonewall had reached as far south as Tidewater
by the time Joe found himself away from home as a college freshman. But they were only ripples. Joe stepped out of the closet and
into a world of rigid sexual segregation. The new giddy confidence
of gay liberation lay thinly over a society still full of old straight
threat and old gay tradition.

When Joe came out in the early 1970s, he possessed an innate
self-confidence and the self-esteem of a six-four stud who spent
summers working on his father's construction sites. Freedom was
new and sweet. Joe could, and did, flame. In fact, Joe was flaming
so furiously he needed to stop, drop, and roll. On the campus of a
small, religiously affiliated college, he created quite a stir.

Of course, being out, even in so small a community, saved a great deal of time. In the dying days of the closet, the sexually segregated society mingled in rest rooms, dirty-book stores, and dark parks. Through a complicated series of signals, potential partners recognized each other. If you were openly out, at least half of that silent communication was unnecessary.

In one of Joe's classes was a hunky ex-marine returning to school on the GI Bill. Joe opened the front door to his apartment one afternoon to this guy's knock. They quickly found themselves in bed, and, almost as quickly, Joe's classmate/lover moved out of the place he shared with two straight guys and in with Joe.

The former roommates found Joe between classes and told him that if he didn't encourage Joe's new lover to move back in with them, they would tell the ex-marine that he was living with a god-damn queer. Showing a great deal of restraint on behalf of the boyfriend, Joe told the ex-roommates that the guy knew all about him, without outing the boy to his buddies.

As with most lovers at the age of eighteen, Joe and the ex-marine had a lot of intense sex briefly and burned out spectacularly, without the help of straight roommates. But beyond that romance lay the greater gay world where so many other lovers were waiting, the Sunday afternoon tea dances, and also disco.

It was all about hair and clothes. No self-respecting Southern queer boy went out tacky or without every layered hair sprayed solidly in place. Friday and Saturday nights, Joe and his friends would drive long distances to the nearest clubs, places where boys could dance together, in front of God and everybody, in Raleigh, in Greenville, in Chapel Hill, and in Norfolk. Every weekend Joe joined the cavalcade of queers racing between cities.

Dancing was for fun. Tricking was for real. No more having to tap your foot in a freezing toilet by the side of the road somewhere. No, you could cruise and drink and smooch before going home to fuck like dogs with each shining Saturday night's star.

This was a heady period for Joe. In the endless weekend traveling, friends were found as readily as lovers. Lovers became friends. Friends became family. It was all new and daring and fun. No malady surfaced that a course of amoxicillin or a bottle of Kwell couldn't cure. The heart wasn't yet hardened by the constant emotional and sexual roulette.

Joe's aim as an early disco twink was to have fun, get drunk, dance, and hopefully get laid. Not yet fully untethered from the notions of union and marriage he had lived with all his life, he began and ended a series of relationships that lasted weeks or months. It took years for the expectations of romance and marriage in a gay form to become callused by his efforts to meet them.

In childhood he looked for someone to be cowboys with. That search only became subsumed by the sustained failure of the search and the promise of unending variety. It became pointless to spend so much emotional energy on the mere quest for sex. The world had accommodatingly arrived at a point where more was better. Joe, the gatherer of love and experience, became a hunter. Saturday night stopped being a search for love and became a hunt for multiple cum-stained memories.

Like most gay men who came out in the early 1970s, Joe held somewhat to the notion that, as a group, we needed to redefine a morality that didn't apply to us as a minority. For any minority, power lies in instinctive exploitation of the majority's desires and fears. With our identities threatened and despised, gay men developed a keen instinct for the sublimated desires and fears of the larger culture and used them to remorselessly bludgeon our way into social significance.

Gay men's definition of themselves became almost entirely experiential. In lieu of a hated identity forced on them by a culture that alternately exploited and dismissed them, gay men began to define themselves by a single-minded hunt for sexual experience.

However, the accumulation of experience leaches innocence from a fertile ground. When the stuff of dreams is acquired in fact and consumed in haste, emotional fulfillment is diluted. The thrill of the hunt and its expression of raw power become satisfying substitutes for emotional fulfillment. Eventually the hunt becomes more important than the kill.

One year, Joe came back from the winter furniture market in High Point. This event draws interior designers, merchandisers, and manufacturers' reps from all over the nation, if not the world, to an otherwise sleepy industrial town in the North Carolina Piedmont.

For gay men, it is also a gathering of the tribes. The furniture market is a professional event; it is also a sexual market of incredible opportunity and diversity. Joe came back in high spirits, victorious in all his many conquests. Exhausted, but satiated and exhilarated, Joe returned to our barren little corner of the world with stories of a sexual binge that seemed as if downtown Manhattan had reincarnated itself in sleepy High Point. The business of business seemed to have become a side attraction in a carnival of sex.

It was only a few years later that the hunt turned calculated and began to mean something different altogether. After a year of spectacular setbacks, both emotionally and fiscally, Joe was offered a position as producer-director for a production of *Sweeney Todd: The Demon Barber of Fleet Street,* in another port city in southern North Carolina.

Not as large as Norfolk, but still possessing the same randy inclinations under a thin skin of propriety, Wilmington is an open city for queers. Sailors and fisherman come to it from the sea. Horny farm boys and soldiers follow the river down from the cotton, corn, and tobacco fields or the bases and military reservations of lower North Carolina. Tourists flood in from an entire region of cities, towns, spots, and places, all on annual holiday. Wilmington is heaven on earth for queers in the summertime.

Joe strode into this city of opportunity with the promise of a long overdue personal success and the hunger born of a long period of emotional starvation. Away from an identity grown stale at home, Joe was able to re-create himself for a brief while and exercise the power of a hunter. Many years later, I asked him about that time. Joe looked away across a hard-won expanse of lawn that signified his long transition back to the role of gatherer. "I became a sexual predator," he said simply.

The term has terrible connotations, but not from obvious assumptions in this application. The words "sexual predator" evoke images of the child molester or serial rapist. That is a correct association in some cases, but not in Joe's. For gay men, survivors of the age of AIDS, the term sexual predator carries with it all the menace of the gay hunter who has moved into a sexual realm free of guilt or a sense of consequence. It is the end result of a gatherer's transition to a hunter, his growing intoxication with the exercise of absolute sexual power.

A person becomes a sexual predator out of hatred. It can be self-hatred or social hatred or a combination of both. The sexual predator has left the association between sex and emotion far behind. Very little humanity is left in the exercise of instinct and pure will. There is, however, a tremendous sense of focus and grim self-satisfaction.

As with any other disassociative state, only two results can occur; consequences assert themselves. There is death or redemption from destruction. In some very real ways, Joe was destroyed by one summer season as a consummate sexual predator. From the destruction, he rebuilt himself in a return to the role of a gatherer. He found a lover and gathered him into an increasingly rich life. He retains the skill of the hunter, but with the wisdom that comes with it, he chooses not to exercise the skills.

Joe hunted in the fields of his own kind. It was a rich hunting ground. So many gay men are willing sheep, placidly offering their emotional throats to the teeth of a faithless wolf. Predator and prey dance a pas de deux of circular roles, now hunting, then hunted. Sexual roles are not engraved in stone beyond the bedrock of fundamental desires.

The bedrock of my fundamental desires is different from Joe's. Yet, I learned the basics of the sexual hunt from his lore and example, that sex could involve a sense of freedom and liberation. By the time I met him, Joe was a master hunter. From him, I also learned that sexual aggression was a part of gay male identity.

Always a pretty boy, I was only experienced in being pursued and seduced. As a result, I was still in love with the idea of being in love. On one level, I wanted a dumber and stronger twin with whom to match wits and sexual stamina. On quite another, I wanted that tall, dark, quiet man to rescue me and make everything all right. Until I met Joe, all my emotional and erotic energy had been spent looking for those ideals. It was incredibly freeing to learn I could aggressively pursue what I wanted, instead of passively waiting. It was as heady as landing a punch solidly in the gut of an opponent.

Yet, I wasn't willing to settle for the variety in which Joe found solitary solace. In many ways, I found the world he showed me to be tawdry and jaded. I also had no desire for gay men. My sexual taste ran to Sandy and his daddy, even as the futility of loving straight men became increasingly real. I didn't know that I would soon come to use the lessons he was teaching when the frustrations of my own search deadened my pure intent. I would have a different prey.

An old saying states, "Be careful what you wish for; you may get it." I got Sandy. That story comes later, but in the anger and emotional numbness of his loss, I became a sexual predator as well. In some sense, I knew exactly what I was doing. I enacted a great deal of psychic revenge on straight men who showed me their throats. Like Joe, I came to like the taste of power, and emotional blood. But I was far more vicious than he ever was or wanted to be.

There is a certain area behind the gay bars of Raleigh and Greenville, North Carolina. Probably similar areas can be found behind gay bars across the South. Gay bars are an urban phenomenon; they are usually located in poor neighborhoods or industrial areas out of obvious sight of "decent" people. Those areas are like a motorized meat market, as men too shy or too afraid to enter the bars drive in circles around the locus of their curiosity and desire. At once fearful and daring, they can no more resist the attraction than moths beating their way around a back porch light.

In endless circles they drive on those streets with half-opened windows and searching eyes. Spotting something they like, they pursue the object of their desire with driving skills akin to the talent of Richard Petty or Dale Earnhardt. Following this vehicular tango the pursuer and pursued end up side by side in a deserted area. A lingering look becomes a jerked-up chin. An answering, knowing grin leads quickly to sex.

So I found myself a regular on that circuit. I had no patience for the niceties of meeting gay men in the bars. I didn't want to seduce them or fuck them. I wanted the furtive young breeder boys and men, sporting eyes full of fear under the pulled low brims of their baseball caps. I could smell their hunger under their honest sweat and cheap aftershave. I knew their loneliness and what simple tenderness lay under the hard twist of their mouths and curt nods. They were so easy to have. They were so easy to have and let go. They couldn't hurt me, not like I'd been hurt. I had all the power in the world over them. It was sweet.

I remember one guy, good-looking and driving a company truck. After letting him chase me for a half hour, I pulled up beside a darkened warehouse. He pulled up next to me. He rolled down his window and said he was looking for some pot. I told him that wasn't what I was looking for and I didn't have any to sell. He asked me what I was looking for. I grinned. He opened the passenger side door and said, "Get in."

We talked a little bit. He said he was married and had two kids. He was just stuck out of town, and lonesome. I asked him if he'd ever . . . He shook his head and looked out his window. He looked back and asked me if I wanted to. I glanced back at the bed of the truck. It was empty. He nodded and opened his door.

Snared, his dick was hard as a sixteen-year-old's; struggling, so was his first kiss; surrendering, he fucked like a cornered man. The sex was a like a fistfight, furious elbows and knees, bruising and biting.

I drew in his maleness, the harsh beard scratch and soft hair of him. I drained the strength from his heavy muscles' straining. I stole his baby-making cum. I wanted to leave him spent and battered and half dead from giving in to what he dreaded and wanted. It was me. I was the one who could tear him from his smug, bitch-fucking arrogance. He wanted me. I took him down.

He finished and fell over me like a dead weight. I stroked the long, sweat-slicked length of his back with a victor's pity and looked up for the stars. The sky was empty and black. He pushed himself off me abruptly and began looking for his clothes in the dark.

It didn't take me long to pull on my shorts and sneakers. I hadn't worn a shirt. I put on his baseball cap and handed him his boots. He looked up at me as he sat on the tailgate and undid the laces left tied in the rush of attack. Even in the dark I could see his fear, hatred, and disgust. As I turned to go back to my car, he said, "You know I'm going to try my best to forget I ever saw your goddamn face, don't you?"

I turned around and pulled the bill of his cap down low over my eyes. I said, "It don't matter. You weren't man enough to make me remember you." I got in my car. I looked back at him sitting, looking down at a boot in his hand. I laughed out loud. I cranked the car and drove off, laughing still.

I played that game for a while. The backseat of my car was littered with baseball caps. Finally, my own meanness started to eat me alive. My laughter began to sound slightly demented, even to me. I quit driving around hunting for straight guys. I drew up tight and closed myself off from the night. I stopped feeling anything for years before I forgave myself and I began to forgive Sandy. I retired my hunting skills. I tended my scars and let the killing fields of desire grow fallow and fecund for something richer to grow.

One night, not long after Jeff and I moved into our new neighborhood, I had to go to the grocery store. Out of cigarettes, out of beer, out of milk—I don't recall. I do know Jeff wanted a special kind of bottled iced tea. That had to be a fairly urgent need for me to leave the house so late. I made a left-hand turn into the grocery store's parking lot behind a truck making a right.

I ended up parking nose to nose with the truck. In the brief brightness of the headlights, the driver and I locked eyes. Before I cut the lights and the engine, I saw the driver was a guy about my age.

As he got out of his truck, our eyes met briefly, before I busied myself getting out of my Bronco. The guy hesitated while I got out and locked my door. When I looked up, he looked away quickly and strode toward the door. Following him into Publix, I noticed he was tall, dark, and sweaty. His T-shirt clung to his back. It rode up in damp folds above the rolling swell of his ass, obvious even in baggy basketball shorts.

At the Ten Items or Less checkout register, I found myself behind the guy once more. The checkout girl swept his twelve-pack of Bud and a box of Pampers across the sensor. Though he didn't stink in the grocery store's frigid air-conditioning, I could smell him. He smelled familiar. I dismissed all this, as I'd trained myself to do since Jeff and I became serious. Noticing any looks or lone males who came my way was only reflex action by now, quickly mentally filed away where the temptations have no power and fantasy stews stickily in the dark.

This guy wasn't even a fantasy. He was just another suburban breeder, stopping at the store after his workout for the beer his wife forgot. Well-trained, he remembered the Pampers. My new neighborhood was full of guys just like him. Buttoned-down and pressed during the day, for awhile each night, these guys grew rangy and rank with testosterone on basketball and tennis courts or soccer fields. Alone, they moved like solitary dogs, sneaking out of the house to roam with a memory of wildness before home, supper, and sleep.

I put him out of my mind as he walked out the door. I paid for my items and made my way out to the near-empty parking lot. The breeder guy was putting his stuff in the back of his truck. As I walked up to my Bronco, he turned and caught my eye. I nodded noncommittally, like you do when you want to be both pleasant and dismissive.

Ignoring any response, I opened my door, tossed my stuff in the back, and climbed into the driver's seat. As I looked up from putting the key in the ignition, I noticed him looking at me still. With a slightly cruel smile, he held my eyes while he stripped off his T-shirt and tossed it into the back of his truck. Reaching for the door handle, he pointedly rearranged his dick before opening the door and climbing into the cab.

I cranked up the Bronco and turned on the headlights. In the quick glare illuminating the inside of his truck, the guy lifted his chin abruptly in invitation. He cranked up his truck, and in his answering headlights' glare, instinctively, my chin lifted in acknowledgment.

He backed up slowly, looking at me as long as he could. When his truck was pointed head out and put in drive, I backed up so that my headlights were pointed in the same direction. He pulled away slowly, using an unnecessary turn signal as he steered his truck toward the grocery store's empty, dark, back lot. I watched him drive well out of any light and then back his truck into a parking space. He killed his headlights.

My mouth was dry. My heart was beating with a heavy thud. Along with a tightening in my shorts grew a slithery longing in my chest. I could already taste his sweat. I could feel the heaviness of him in my hand. I could feel his hands between my legs, at the back of my neck. I didn't need to look for this man waiting in the dark; I could have found him by scent and desire alone.

Like a hundred other nights before that one, all my focus was centered on that scent. It blew in my window with the hot, heavy breeze. It clung to the music from the radio, licking me with the notes of a song. I wondered, how many years has it been since I followed the jerk of a chin and a horny grin into a dark public spot and a darker vehicle?

It wasn't that I didn't want to do it again; there was no need. I knew how it ended. This sweaty somebody's daddy, somebody's husband, somebody's boyfriend wasn't even a stranger. He was every boy I ever knew, with a hundred first names, but no last ones. In some ways, I began and ended in a truck like that one, the dark smelling of sweat, tasting like semen, and revealing the unexpected tenderness in a stranger's haunted eyes.

I looked at the clock. Jeff was waiting a few blocks away for his favorite bottled tea and cigarettes. I looked back through the dark to the darker shape of the waiting truck. I felt the old power and meanness quicken and surge after a long sleep.

Quickly a cab light came on and went off. I watched as he moved toward the opposite side of his truck and leaned back against the quarter panel, cupping his crotch with one hand, rubbing his chest with the other. I laughed. The predator turned the other way and headed home. Still laughing, the gatherer didn't look back.

Chapter 7

The Importance of Dancing

One bright Saturday evening in June, Joe and I took off at sunset for the ninety-minute drive to Norfolk's gay bars. It was my first time. I had never before made it past the door to any gay bar. I went to a gay bar once as an undergrad and made it through the front door, only to be confronted by a sign that stated baldly that this was a gay club open to members and their guests only. Standing before that sign, I was in a quandary. I didn't know anyone to be a guest of. I was too scared to "join." I was vaguely afraid that buying a membership would put my name on some secret federal queer list.

I turned around and left that club without even making it past the vestibule. I had no way of knowing that membership was a formality to comply with North Carolina's Byzantine liquor laws. There was also no way for me to know that the doorman was a member and anyone who wanted to get in without a membership was automatically his "guest." It would be a long time before I was to discover that there was no "federal" queer list and that the greater world of authority really didn't give a damn what you did unless it needed to either exploit you or make a scapegoat of you.

My earlier fear of associating with known homosexuals was rapidly diminishing before the promise of sex and romance in Joe's collection of bar lore. Joe had decided it was high time I went dancing. I was definitely ready. I had been an avid dancer throughout high school and college at all of the straight bars. I wasn't one bit shy. I could funk and bump and shake my groove thang with the best of them. I had just grown tired of feigning interest in and buying beers for some girl just so I had a dance partner. Now, Joe was telling me it was my turn.

I can still taste the sweet wind and bitter diet pills we took as we raced in Joe's black Cutlass over the bridge into the lights of the port city. Norfolk was the black harbor, with hulking ships and steaming shipyards, the tall buildings beckoning like the straddling legs of a giant sailor churning promises up from under his swaggering feet.

Past the echoing lights of Portsmouth and onto the street, we passed the tired straight people trudging sleepily out of Harborside to go home. Our night was just beginning. WOWI was blasting that summer's crop of love and love-gone-wrong songs as we swept around the edge of the water toward Freemason Harbor and the first stop of the night. The cheap speed made me grit my teeth and watch, as all the motion and music and color came to a stop in a dingy parking lot just off Granby Street. Across the way was the Boiler Room.

Dark, smoky, dirty, and seedy beyond time, the Boiler Room was on the first floor of a downtown transient hotel that catered to port-stranded mariners. The Seaman's Lodge and the Boiler Room had somehow escaped the face-lift perpetrated on Norfolk's waterfront area. It was uncompromisingly sinister, positioned as it was on a sleazy side street just beyond the phony yuppie optimism glittering on the waterfront.

Joe strode into the bar as if he owned it and me. With a proprietary air, he steered me to the long bar that ran down one side of the joint into darkness. He ordered us both a beer and, on getting them, promptly abandoned me to go pee. I needed the beer bad to take the edge off the speed, which had kicked in with a particularly sharp glint to it. Sitting on a bar stool, I gazed across the bar to the dirty mirror behind the liquor bottles and found my face looking frightened and pale. I had to smile back at myself. I looked like a twelve-year-old in a whorehouse.

I pulled my eyes away from that image and turned my back to the bar to check out the room. The obligatory pool table and a jukebox revealed themselves in the sharp clatter of a cannonball break and gaudy Wurlitzer lights between the densely packed bodies of men. These were men. There wasn't a preppy or clean-cut face in the room. No, these guys were as menacing as the street, despite their ages. It was a tough room.

Leather guys were bunched in tight knots of stinking hides and glinting chains. Their bushy mustaches looked dated, like the woman who never abandoned her high school hairstyle. Long-legged guys in Levi's and flannel were rocking back a little on their high-heeled boots. Bodybuilders gleamed, appearing eerily jaundiced or hellish under the yellow and red overhead lights. Some guys who couldn't seem to make up their minds were dressed in hybrids of subculture couture as though expanding their chances by attempting crossover appeal.

Nonetheless, the gathering realization pooled from my groin to my consciousness. These were my people. I was one of them. It comforted and terrified me simultaneously. I was at once alien and at home. Grinning stupidly, I turned back toward the bar.

The dark-haired bartender with the Elgin Marble chest framed between two open panels of his flannel shirt leaned toward me with a grin. I thought he was trying to say something to me over the music so I leaned in to hear, only to see that he was reaching into the beer cooler underneath the bar. He rose quickly and slammed a cold bottle of Bud on the bar in front of me. "Compliments of the guy at the end of the bar, handsome," he said with a grin.

"Which one?" I asked, but he had moved on. I twisted the cap off the bottle and looked into the dimness at the end of the room. A lanky good-looking guy raised his bottle in acknowledgment. I raised mine back. He grinned and started negotiating his way through the crowd toward my end of the bar. I watched him with growing interest as he approached me with a mock-exasperated lifting of his brows and rolling of his eyes. I liked that. He insinuated himself next to me and put one foot up on the bar rail behind me, melding his groin somehow into the incline of my waist. I liked that better.

There was a lot I liked about him. I don't remember much of his come-on, except it was smooth and gleamed in his dark eyes. I was enjoying just talking shit with him, his arm around my shoulders and his crotch grinding steadily into my side. Then Joe reappeared from the bathroom, a knot of older guys following along behind him like a propelling fist in his back. Joe said something along the lines of not being able to leave me alone for a minute.

My admirer warily loosened his hold around my shoulders. Joe's group of acquaintances teased the guy with the edgy familiarity that comes from long association. They warned me he was a dick hound.

They speculated on how Joe came to have me along with him that night. These self-assured, cliquish guys spoke around us as if we were foreigners and didn't quite understand English.

Never one to let a dramatic opportunity go unexploited, Joe told them I was his son. In the rise of music behind the sudden stilled chatter, my admirer took off. The guys who were left drew closer in mute examination, as if Joe and I had unexpectedly changed before their eyes, suddenly imbued with some kind of greater significance.

One middle-aged guy, slightly paunched and trendily leathered, gave me a long, critical appraisal. I half expected him to pry open my mouth and examine my teeth. He said to Joe, "He's got pretty dimples. Can I fuck him?" Joe laughed and said, "Ask him. He's old enough to look out for himself." The guy reached out to pinch my nipple, and I retreated from his hand as far as the bar at my back would allow. I endured his companionable tweak as he asked, "Can I fuck you, baby?"

I was decidedly not having it. The man was condescending and arrogant. I hated his dirty little attitude. Besides, this guy was grossing me out. I looked at Joe. He was waiting to see how I'd handle myself. I looked at my leather daddy and said sweetly, "Do you have any money?" He said, "Plenty. Why?" I gave him a great big smile with a lot of dimple action and said, "Because I don't fuck old people for free."

Joe and the leatherman's clique fell out laughing. My erstwhile seducer said, "Do you shave with that razor tongue?" Which made Joe laugh even more. I felt halfway nauseated, but victorious at the same time. It was like being a little kid playing hide and seek and eluding the kid who was IT to make it home free. Very socially adept at this milieu, Joe smoothed things over with conversation while I said nothing, sipped on my beer, and enjoyed my first taste of being young, desirable, and a bit of a bitch.

Joe continued to weave an ornate, yet plausible, story of his paternity for his curious audience while I just smiled. Finally, I said, "Look, Daddy, let's go somewhere else. I'm over this place." Joe said, "Okay, son, let me finish this beer." Finally, we left to head to the bars in Ghent.

In the car, I lit my eighteenth Marlboro of the night and said, "Where in the hell did you come up with the daddy bit?" Joe just laughed and threw the car into reverse. He turned up the radio and said, "I'm in the mood for a good drag show. Let's go to the Cue." I was up for anything after the Boiler Room.

We hit the street not knowing we had just created an enduring identity for ourselves in the gay demimonde of Norfolk. We became known as that Joe Riddick and his gay son from Nags Head who went out cruising together. For years afterward, Joe would find himself in a bar conversation with someone whose eyes would show a flash of recognition before asking, "Hey. What's your kid up to these days?" But that was all to come later. This night held more myth making in store.

Over by Old Dominion University, the Cue Club drew a different crowd altogether than the Boiler Room. Back then, the Cue drew a mix of black and white, E-1 sailors, and students. As filled with tawdry flash and glitter as the Boiler Room was dark and menacing, the Cue also had a dance floor. The Boiler Room was a cruise bar. Only the seriously fucked up danced in there.

I could feel the bass making the pavement tremble under my sneakers when we got out of the car. By the time we made it to the door, some song was on that made me pull Joe inside like a kid at a carnival. I dragged him onto the dance floor and we danced. I remember grinning, laughing, snapping my fingers, and clapping my hands like I had been born again into the church of disco.

Joe threw back his head and laughed and sang along with me. I will never forget the grin on his face as we gave ourselves up to the sheer happiness in becoming woven into the texture of sound and motion all around us. The freedom was in my ass and my hips. I lifted my hands up to Jesus, grateful for the night and the buzz and my most excellent friend Joe. All around me, the grins and whoops seemed communal, righteous, and joyful. We all shared sweat and poppers as we chanted, "If you don't want to get it on, take your dead ass home!"

Yes, Lord. We sang and we laughed with a fullness that had stayed stunted and bound in our chests through times of aching cold and long hurt. Not anymore. No, not ever again. It was so fucking beautiful. The whole room was beautiful, and I ground my teeth with the sheer intensity of it. Feet, step, move, slide. Ass high up and haughty. Backbone loose and limber enough; legs strong enough to make promises of squeezing a long sigh from deep inside your groin. I didn't want it to stop. Sweet Jesus, it was so good to be young and glittering in music and summer sweat.

But it did stop. The last bass note dimmed to nothing as a show tune paean came up over the speakers. The dancers shook the last bit of rhythm from their fingertips and headed off the dance floor. "What the fuck happened?" I asked Joe. He said, "It's time for the show. You want a beer? Wait right here and hold this spot so we can see."

With that he was gone, leaving me just off the dance floor with a crowd growing at my back. I heard anticipatory murmurs under the too loud, cheesy Broadway music. The lights dimmed and the mirror ball began to throw its splintered spell over the room's eager faces. Joe made it back with our beers just as the invisible emcee announced the evening's first entertainer.

Drag may have been around since ancient times, but this was the 1980s in Norfolk, not ancient Rome. With all the lingering hurt and resentment of someone who had been told most of his life that he was too pretty to be a boy, it was too much for me. I felt vaguely unclean even looking at the first set of heavily made-up drag queens who graced the stage-cum-dance floor.

In their display of exaggerated femininity, I felt myself tighten my hold on the carefully crafted masculinity that I had bought with long years of rigid practice. In their pretereloquence and exaggerated sorrowful lip-synching, I was confronted with all of the shameful shortcomings of my boyhood. I hated them. I wanted to get as far away as possible from the crowd's reverent offerings of dollar bills tucked into these creatures' tortured cleavage or grasped tightly in their slender fingers tipped with battle-length Lee Press-On Nails.

Behind me, the crowd cheered and applauded wildly. Beside me, Joe shouted, "Work it, Miss Thing!" I applauded noncommittally as each set ended and the entertainer carefully stepped off the stage in size fifteen heels. Then, all the houselights dimmed to darkness. Almost prayerfully, the emcee stated simply, "Ladies and Gentleman . . . Miss Tawny Ross-Bofill."

This was the summer when Jennifer Holiday tore at the airwaves with her hit from the Broadway musical *Dreamgirls.* Now, if deep in the heart of every gay man is the half-healed scar of that one painful lost love, it seems to take a black woman to give it a voice. Defiance, passion, anger, despair, and a sexual attraction that would make you crawl across broken glass—all are concentrated every few years into a sort of gay anthem. That summer, Jennifer Holiday raised a voice like smoke-smudged silver to hold the anthem high.

In the scant seconds between the silence following the announcement of the name Tawny Ross-Bofill and the opening sustained violin strum of the song, there was a collective intake of breath. Simultaneously, the lights came up to reveal a lone, skinny, black girl who lifted her head and sang, "And I am telling you . . . I'm not going . . . " The crowd behind me blew up.

Gangly Navy boys betrayed by their haircuts, and students betrayed by theirs, opened their voices in a howl of adoration and empathy. The tiny figure onstage became animated, no, possessed, by the pathos of the song. She writhed, she emoted, she lived the song before our very eyes and, in doing so, expressed the depths of our own heartbreaks and resolute resiliency.

We called that scrawny heifer back for three encores. What I had seen before her was what Joe called "booger drag." Miss Tawny Ross-Bofill was theater. When she was finally led, devastated and exhausted, from the stage by a couple of shirtless stud "bodyguards," I turned to Joe, speechless. He chuckled and leaned down to tell me in my ear that she was regionally famous. She was the holder of several titles, such as "Miss Tri-State Entertainer of the Year" (Southern drag queens are more competitive than debutantes and more self-congratulatory than country music stars). In reality, it was said, she was a tiny man who supported his drag career as a transvestite prostitute and had a fabulous apartment in the Hague Towers.

I was overwhelmed. The music came back on and Joe told me to drink up. It was time to go to the Late Show. We did another hit of speed, drank our beers, and left the Cue Club. So far, I had enjoyed being out. It was nice being hit on by the guy who bought me a beer at the Boiler Room. The Cue Club had extended the joy of communal dancing and more than a bit of education in another facet of queer culture. But so far, the evening hadn't produced any romance.

I hadn't seen any fantasies become flesh; I hadn't seen anybody I wanted to fuck, anyway.

We drove the short distance to the Late Show, with the second hit of speed coming in more brightly than the first. Through Joe's explanation of how the Late Show got its name and what I could expect, I wondered if I was cut out for this life. In the middle of so much sudden experience, I felt the speed make me edgy and a little sad. I didn't say anything. Deciding to give it all a fair shot, I settled in for the ride.

It is part of my nature when presented with way too much information to sort of shut down until I can absorb it all. By 2 a.m. that night, I had reached that point on entering the Late Show. Joe wanted to wander around and check stuff out. I just wanted to go somewhere and stare. We stopped off at the bar. Joe got another beer and I got water. The speed was drying me out. After a few minutes, we split up to cruise around on our own.

The Late Show was different from all the other clubs because its membership was the most expensive and it didn't even open until 2 a.m. when all the other clubs closed. It was cavernous. It had a restaurant, at least three bars I can recall, and an outside area with a volleyball court. Despite all that, the first night I went with Joe, I was really sort of underwhelmed by it at first.

I wandered outside and perched myself on a picnic table, feigning interest in the volleyball game going on. I looked up into the night sky. The stars were blotted out by the haze of city smoke trapped in humidity and reflecting mercury vapor streetlights. The wind came up, but it was cooling. Slowly, I surfaced over the top of the speed and my own weirdness.

Looking around, I noticed a studly guy pass by a couple of times. He was my height, but a total mesomorph. Dressed only in a pair of loose camouflage pants and a pair of high-top sneakers, he moved with the solid ease of rounded muscle. His hair was cut high and tight over surprisingly small ears. He had to be a marine with that haircut and that build. I felt a stab of lust that surprised me. I dismissed it, reluctantly.

Feeling centered again, I pushed up off the picnic table and headed inside to find Joe. Over by the dance floor, I caught sight of him dancing with some guy. He looked as if he was having a pretty good time, so I figured I'd just hang out and wait for him to come off the dance floor.

The deejay fired up the long version of "Don't You Want Me?" by the Human League. I loved that song. I was just standing there wishing I could dance when I felt someone come up beside me. It was the marine from outside. I sort of smiled and he nodded back before staring out onto the dance floor with a fierce look of concentration. I blew it off. No big deal, until he turned and leaned into my ear and shouted, "You want to dance?" I nodded and he caught me by my upper arm and half dragged me onto the dance floor with an almost grim look on his face.

With the song wrapping itself between us and around us, he looked at me and smiled quickly. I smiled back and looked off into that middle distance your eyes seek when you are dancing with somebody you don't really know. When I looked back, I realized this guy was still looking at me. The crowd had pushed us closer together. I could see a bead of sweat gather in the hollow of his throat and slide down his chest.

I backed up some to give him more room. He moved in closer, following my retreat. Bumping my ass against a dancer behind me, I stepped into my partner. I looked up to acknowledge my invasion of his personal space and found his eyes boring into mine. It was a challenge. It was a question.

I responded by fitting myself into him, my thigh between his legs, his thigh between mine. I moved my head into the crook of his neck. We were touching nowhere but our chests and the moving thump of thigh to taint. He put his hand in the small of my back and pulled me deeper into him. I responded by licking the sweat from his Adam's apple up to his chin.

He tilted his head back and closed his eyes. I put one hand on his waist and one at the back of his head. We slowed against the insistence of the beat. Grinding, dipping, he bent his knees to help me ride his thigh.

As the Human League played out, the unearthly chords of Africa Bambaataa's "Planet Rock" unfolded and stretched out like a summons from outer space. My marine took the hem of my T-shirt and lifted it over my head. Without missing a beat he tucked my shirt into the back of the waistband of his trousers, before pulling me into the smooth slickness of his chest. As the technofunk rolled apoca-lyptically down on us, he kissed me suddenly, hard on the mouth. I opened my lips to allow the desperately sweet, hot fullness of his tongue.

Without warning he pushed me away, only to grab me by my hips, turn me around, and pull me back again. He held onto me with one palm against my right nipple and the other hand tucked into the waistband of my shorts, palm flat against my belly. Hot and sweat-slicked, he moved against my back. I could feel his hard dick pushing at the crack of my ass through the cloth of our pants. He moved into me relentlessly, moving his hand farther down into my shorts to shelter the length of my hardening dick in his palm.

This wasn't dancing. This wasn't a communal rite of liberation. This was something else altogether. This was a good slow fuck on the dance floor. Earlier, I had given in to the happiness and joy of the music. Now I let it move me into the hard chest and under the strong hand of this man behind me. I fit myself hungrily to his thrusts. The only thing that separated me from his total possession was a few layers of cloth.

Awkwardly, he pressed his mouth into my shoulder. Even over the echoing throb of the music, I could hear the quickening of his breath. As he battered me from behind, he tightened his possession of my dick. I felt myself start to quicken and loosen inside, the ethereal music letting the slow glide of landing begin as I got close to cumming.

Then the song was over, and another one began. My marine let me go and stepped away from behind me, leaving my wet back exposed to a cold blast of air-conditioning and my dick painfully tenting my shorts. I turned around to find him rearranging himself in his pants. He grinned sheepishly as he took my shirt from his waistband and wiped his face. Extending it back to me, he said, "That was pretty hot. You got me real close, ya know?"

He motioned his head for us to leave the dance floor. Just off it and into the unconcerned crowd, he kissed me quickly and said, "Are you going to hang out for awhile?" I said, "Maybe." He looked around, caught someone's eye, and jerked up his chin in greeting. He looked back at me hurriedly and said, "Want to do some MDA?" I said, "No." He nodded and said, "Maybe we can hook up later. It's still pretty early." I said, "Sure." He gave me another quick kiss on the mouth and was gone.

I looked around and saw Joe looking at me with a mixture of amusement and concern. I walked over to him and he said in greeting, "Well. You certainly put on a show. Getting dry humped on the dance floor by a marine on your first night out. Son, I am scared of you."

I grinned as if I had just come through an obtuse, but grueling, initiation with flying colors. "We need to be thinking about getting on back to the beach," he said. I looked around for my marine. He was nowhere to be seen. "Let him go, baby," Joe said. "There's always somebody else hotter. Now, let's go get us some breakfast. You have got to check out the Colley Café at 4 a.m. There's this drag queen waitress with a really nasty attitude . . ."

We did indeed go to the Colley Café, though the drag queen waitress was in a good mood. Driving burned out back to the beach in the gathering light down US 158, all I could think of was how I had met a really hot guy, fallen in love, gotten mostly laid, and been abandoned all in the space of two extended dance mixes. I knew I would be going back for more.

That became many nights over the course of years, each of them distilled from that single night. Like a born drunk is lost to one shot of liquor, I became lost in the music and the lights and the feel of a marine's sweaty hand down my pants and his beer-scented breath in my ear.

The routine rarely varied, except occasionally we went to the Oarhouse instead of the Cue Club. As I grew more confident cruising on my own, Joe and I separated sooner. Often we would meet a trick at the bar, agree to meet at the Colley Café at 4 a.m. for breakfast, and then go home with them. My marine was a onetime deal, but I did discover the charms of navy personnel. Over time, my tricks got older and Joe's got younger.

Once, we split with our respective finds to hook up later for the ride home. I had met a tall drink of water from Texas who was a commander on a sub. He took me to his place and made a substantial impression on my opinion of both the navy and the Republic of Texas. Joe had picked up a sort of scruffy blond who was a demon

in bed. Turns out that guy was a Virginia Beach vice cop who did
queer patrol in shore toilets.

We all met after some memorable sex for a more memorable
breakfast at the Colley Café. Joe's cop found a roach crawling up
the wall next to him and freaked out like a little girl. Obviously
bemused and disturbed by his breakfast companions, my navy commander gallantly picked up my check and booked. I don't remember if we ever saw either one of them again, but I don't think we'll
ever forget them.

What lingers as the lesson is the dancing. In that movement and
heady beat lay all the gold and dross of freedom and sex. From
liberation to seduction to a gritty sexual confidence, Joe led me to
Norfolk and initiated me into the gay fraternity of the disco.

The time would come when my attitude was so finely crafted that
Joe would shout to me as we danced, "Smile!" By then, dancing
was deadly serious—my face pulled into a haughty arrogance in a
feeble attempt to defend myself against the splinters of the heart
that I picked up off the dance floor.

There was another time, much later. One freezing night back
home on the beach, Joe and I found ourselves in his shop. Long
after hours, we must have stopped by to pick up something. I don't
recall. It was not long after my lover, Rick, left me for the first time.
Joe was putting up with a lot from me in the wake of that leaving.
I was staying high all the time thanks to some sinsemilla, tequila,
and a large cache of black-market Valium. Fortunately, Joe was
staying close enough to catch me if I fell from those numbed
heights of pain.

That night, as Joe busied himself in the cold shop, I turned on the
radio to listen to the great night deejay on WOWI. This guy was
called the Master Storyteller. Over the course of the night's airplay
he wove stories of love and life in between the mix of dance songs
and soul songs. That man was the most soulful, wonderful deejay in
the world. His mellow, blues- and smoke-cured voice was the one
link from old times to that bad time that stayed good to me.

That night, with the wind a steady lonesome howl outside and
cold enough to see your breath inside, the Master Storyteller was
weaving a tale too close to my bone-weary own. Numb for weeks,
his story was bringing me close to tears. Those kind of tears you

don't want to get started. They carve canyons of regret, not release, in their trail. But the Master, man . . . he had the nerve to play this one song to bookend that story. The song was assertive but resigned to a kind of sexual addiction that was still everything I could manage to feel.

The Master dropped the needle on Chaka Kahn singing "Ain't Nobody." As the opening riff chortled into the cold air, I nudged up the volume. Joe was standing by his desk reading some papers. I heard his fingers snap, and I looked up to see him throw back his head and stick out his leg in the unmistakable opening steps of his personal dance.

"Go on. Turn it up," he said, as he reached one hand up in beseeching supplication. I stood and let go all the hurt and anger I had gathered up so carefully. Along with Chaka I began to sing, "Ain't nobody, love me better, make me happy, make me feel this way." In response to my call, Joe echoed in affirmation behind me. Shouting like I was in church, I lifted my hand to testify.

Dancing, Joe and I faced each other to sing along with another black woman who could articulate a queer's longing, lonesomeness, and pain. I danced and sang in testament to something I had and lost. Something I thought nobody was ever going to do for me again. In an echoing gospel shout, Joe opened the door of his own memory and despair in sympathy and communion with my own.

Our voices mingled with Chaka's over the cold night air. My raspy howl of a voice sailing toward Philadelphia, Joe's to God knows where. And we danced, my body moving in the cold under the music's caress and the memory of one man's touch. And we made it over another lonesome night's despair. Did that longing given voice and motion find its way to the ear or heart of its intended, the author of that despair? Like the Master Storyteller used to say, "Ah, but that's another story." We begin and end this one, dancing.

Chapter 8

Lovers

I have become convinced that there are two great loves in everyone's life: the one you love and the one you love to fuck. The greater part of anyone's largest personal drama—pathetic, bathetic, and hubristic—stems from not knowing which one is which. For most of us, the latter precedes the former. In learning the difference, you gain the world after seeming to have lost everything.

The great sexual passion you find first is serendipitous. That lover comes like a sudden breeze over wide still waters, shattering the moon's reflection into a thousand glimmering diamonds. Heedless or uncaring of the possibility of drowning, you dive in to gather the surprise of riches thrown before you like a gift from heaven.

Only later, alone and shivering, do you learn the gift was dispersed by the greed in accepting it. Your hands wet with regret, you move on with a plundered soul. You always look for the bandit in any other lover's eyes who took you for all you sought to take. Heartache isn't just a song on the radio anymore. It has a name.

Joe met Pickett long before me. Pickett is an approximation of his real name. Suffice it to say, he was one of those scions of a broken-down Southern aristocracy who named their children with the last names of dead forebears. Ahhh, but that was no small part of the draw. Joe was a Virginia boy. Nowhere else in the South, with the exception of Charleston, South Carolina, is the attraction of one's heritage so carefully tended and proudly extended as it is in Virginia.

A certain set of characteristics comes along with such an identity. Pickett was the sine qua non of them all. Tall, lean, and dashing, he carried his handsome self as if to the manor born. The broad vowels of old Tidewater dropped from his mouth like honey dripping all over the old plantation.

Carelessly preppy and suitably conversant in all things cultural, he was a dream come true for Joe. Hot, hung, and horny as white trash, Pickett was as at home in a box seat at the opera as he was slung up naked in bed. As with all great passions, we tend to fall in love with a breathing personification of how we see ourselves. Joe went on Pickett like white on rice.

Of course, Pickett personified some of the less desirable traits of the Old Southern rich-boy identity. He had a steady thirst for good bourbon and better gin (depending on the time of day). Alcohol may have lowered his lids to a sexy scowl, but it also brought out the twinned thorns of attraction and repulsion. He didn't mind making a scene, hoping it would lead to a fight. He also would fuck a woodpile if he thought there was a snake underneath it.

Like most survivors of the Great War of Northern Aggression, Pickett's family's riches were more in his mind than in the bank. When Joe met him, Pickett was working as a hotel desk clerk while taking a year off from college. That ruse really translated into the literal fact that he was dumb as a post and his mama and daddy weren't going to support his lazy ass anymore.

In the mirror of hot attraction, Pickett saw Joe as the real deal. Joe had the accent, style, and culture of a Virginia gentleman. He owned a successful business; he drove a nice car; he dressed from the best stores. For a long while, both of them failed to see that the ease of old money was based on the fact that Joe worked his ass off and Pickett didn't.

Worse, Pickett really enjoyed conjuring up a pale imitation of Tallulah Bankhead's antics. He perpetuated enough drama around himself to exhaust even the most adoring lover. Drinking in the dead of winter at the bar of the Kill Devil Hills Holiday Inn, Pickett and Joe sat at the same table with the girlfriend of a Wanchese commercial fisherman. Pickett thought it was cool to neck with this girl to irritate Joe.

Well, it wasn't long before the boyfriend showed up. Now, a Wanchese commercial fisherman is the last in a long line of only four or five families that began their lineages as pirates and wreckers. Three centuries of inbreeding have produced the current crop of progeny who can do three things: fish, fuck, and fight.

For the boyfriend, that night, the fish weren't running and the fucking seemed to be on the wrong side of the bed, so to speak. The last available option was obvious. Imagine this big woolly throw-back coming upon two piss-elegant college boys, one of whom was sucking face with his girlfriend. You can't speculatively narrow eyes that are only a quarter-inch apart.

"Whose this motherfucker you're kissing on, bitch?" The fisherman says. "It's all right, honey. This here Pickett is gay; he don't mean nothing by it," the girlfriend replies.

"Whuudya mean gay? He damn sure ain't gonna mean nothing after I kick his happy ass," the fisherman says. "No, sugar. Pickett don't mean nothing by kissing me. He's queer. That there is his boyfriend, Joe," the girlfriend replies in her best conciliatory voice. She sounds rather like she's trying to talk a mildly retarded three-year-old down from a tree.

With oxlike recognition growing in our fisherman's eyes, he bellows, "Queers? There's queers in here?" Astonished, he looks around the bar for his buddies (who have been buggering each other for years on those six-week treks to the North Atlantic fishing grounds). "Whose gonna come over here and help me kill these faggot sons a bitches?" Pickett looks at Joe and says, "Well, aren't you going to stand up for us?"

Torquing the locals' jaws wasn't limited to bar scenes for Pickett. He got a very real kick out of being as outrageous as possible wherever the opportunity presented itself. Once, a rare blizzard hit the Outer Banks with more than a few feet of snow. At the onset of the storm, the power went out in Kitty Hawk where Joe lived and in Nags Head where Pickett lived. Joe's family's cottage was in the middle of the two, smack dead in the center of Kill Devil Hills.

For some reason, Kill Devil Hills' power didn't go out. As the storm grew, Joe offered shelter to a good friend and neighbor who was home alone with her two young sons. He bundled them up in his car and headed out for his family's place. Normally, the drive would have taken ten minutes at most. That night, buffeted by gale-force winds and heavy blowing snow, the trip took an hour.

Snug in the warm house, Joe was getting his guests settled when the phone rang. It was Pickett. He told Joe he had to come get him. Joe asked him why he couldn't bring himself, an obvious question to ask someone who is six-two, strong, and wiry and who possesses between his legs a rather assertive proof of virility. Unfortunately, the simplicity of the question was lost on Pickett. In fact, it launched a psychodrama of epic proportions, the result of which was a two-hour slog through the storm for Joe to prove his love.

In the quiet of the snowy dawn the following morning, Pickett became possessed with a burning desire to demonstrate his gratitude in a rather intimate way. Joe's heroics, and the presence of a woman and her twelve-year-old and three-year-old boys in the next room, unleashed a passion that included wall banging and screaming. Afterward, Pickett emerged in the presence of his unfortunate audience with a cheery good morning and a request for coffee from Joe's abashed guests.

Joe and Pickett's relationship continued from bed to verse (to steal a phrase), then from bad to worse (to state the obvious). Pickett played the leaving card as his last big scene. Joe let him go. For all the histrionics and historic sex, his exhaustion overcame the effort to maintain a semblance of any sort of normal life.

Joe had his regrets, certainly. In many ways, he really loved Pickett. If he could have cut out the metastasis of melodrama and inherent self-destruction from Pickett's psyche, he would have. But in neutralizing that wildness, what was left but complacency and old age? Adrenaline is addictive.

Pickett let him go through withdrawal for awhile before he reappeared on the beach, begging forgiveness and reunion. Joe said he needed a few days to think about it. At the end of the mulling period, Joe asked Pickett to meet him for dinner so they could talk. Pickett agreed, insisting that they have dinner at the beach's version of haute cuisine, the Sea Ranch.

It was a beautiful evening. The food was excellent. The wine was sweet, and Pickett was on his best behavior. Joe agreed to take him back. They had coffee and cognac while watching the full moon rise over the ocean outside the dining room windows. Deciding to leave, Pickett made much of the reconciliation, stopping at the tables of several acquaintances to announce the good news on their way out.

Feeling expansive and in love, Joe suggested they detour around the back of the dining room to take a walk on the beach before going home and to bed to seal the evening. Once outside, Pickett became pensive and quiet despite his earlier ease and good cheer. On the beach, bathed by the full moon and the cool gleam of lights from the dining room, Pickett looked at Joe and told him he was sorry, he just couldn't do it. Though he loved him, Pickett knew it would never work out.

Joe beat the shit out of him in full view of the diners, looking up from their fish dinners in obvious enjoyment of the evening's grand finale. His anger and humiliation spent, Joe left Pickett bloodied on the beach and drove home alone.

They ran into each other now and then, but never often and never planned. A few years later Joe did plan to meet Pickett and his current boyfriend for dinner in Ghent. Pickett, by that time, had landed in a Virginia Beach condo belonging to a little guy with a big wallet and a bigger appetite for excess than Joe's. The spark that initiated the dinner reunion was me. You see, Pickett is my second cousin on my mama's side.

In the small and large world of Tidewater, Joe and I met and inexplicably suited each other to a T. Only in the long accumulation of coincidences did we both manage to make the association. Pickett and I barely resemble kin. Pickett is a pure example of my mother's gene pool. He is glamourously dark, whereas I am more of a mongrel hybrid of my daddy's blonder people and Mama's people's early easy attraction to native Tuscarora Indian women as practical, hearty, and hardworking wives.

People have often asked Joe and me why we were never lovers. That question has several answers, but I am pretty sure Joe found out Pickett and I were related and quickly slammed the door to any idea of a familial replay.

Still, for all the storm's smoke and thunder surrounding that *coup de foudre,* it is the stories I've just told that Joe most often recalls of his old lovers. I see a certain wistfulness in Joe when Pickett's name comes up. It's a look I recognize from the inside out. Everybody gets struck eventually. Joe watched while I courted the lightning myself and got burned by the same arcing flash again and again.

That storm had a name as well. I'm going to call it Rick, though that isn't his real name, of course. I mentioned to him the idea of writing a book about us a long time ago. Back then, the idea delighted him. He always was a vain son of a bitch. But by now he's been married for over eight years. If his history of fertility is anything to take into account, I'm sure he has kids by now. I don't think he'd be as pleased these days as he was back then.

I wouldn't know. I lost track of him just after he called to say he'd gotten married. That was eight years, almost to the day, after we first met. I guess my voice must have betrayed the insincerity in my congratulations. For once, he tried to make it better. I knew his lying well enough to know he was telling the truth. He told me he never would be as happy as he was just then if it hadn't been for me. He told me I taught him how to really love somebody.

I owe him for that, at least. He told me a long time ago that we knew each other inside and out, top to bottom. For a long time, I knew the contours and hidden dark places of his body and soul as well as he knew mine. We spent a long time surveying to map that intimacy. For whatever else he's got now, he had the first, sweetest piece of me for a long time. I wish him well.

Rick is a good pseudonym for him. It brings to mind that same buccaneer outlaw sexiness that he personified. There is no better name for a guy who played my spermatic chord like Keith Richards plays guitar riffs and then turned me into every song Ricki Lee Jones ever sang. Goddamn, he was the best and the worst I've ever seen. *Après Rick, le déluge.*

We met one spring day not long after I moved back to Kill Devils Hills after an abrupt departure when I discovered I was under surveillance for dealing pot and coke. I had been offered a killer job with an advertising agency that I'd always wanted to work for. I'd cleaned up well. I moved into a tiny beach house on stilts right across the street from where I had lived in the Avalon Beach neighborhood. I loved that house; it was full of sunshine and the promise of happiness.

Life was sweet. I didn't have any intention of fucking up. It was no problem when the chief of police of Nags Head put his hand on my shoulder in the produce aisle of Food Lion and told me he'd be watching me. It was great to be back, hanging out with Joe and doing some really cool work at the ad agency. I was on cruise control.

Just when things were going so well, I caught this guy checking me out in the mirror at the gym. My mama had this saying: "Love is something that comes down from heaven to worry the hell out of you." Heaven was made flesh, and it came down to me in the form of a six-foot, ash-blond-haired, gray-eyed stud doing curls in the free-weight room. He looked like one of Raphael's angels with a dirty grin and a hard-on. Mirror flirting turned into conversation. Conversation led to giving up my address and an exchange of certain questioning and answering looks.

A couple of days later, Rick showed up at my house after work. I heard him before I saw him. He pulled up under my house in a loud-ass, oil-burning, rusted Plymouth Duster held together with Bondo and testosterone. He swung up the steps to the back door on the deck, still damp and salty from a surf session. I let him in and offered him a beer.

We ended up on the couch looking at a drawing I was working on that was lying on the coffee table. This gave him an excuse to sit close enough to me that our thighs were touching. I was starting to sweat. He watched me nervously explain some arcane point I was trying to make in the drawing, those unnerving pale gray eyes never leaving my face. His bare foot found its way over mine, toe by toe until the arch covered it.

I stood up abruptly and so did he. I was suddenly pissed. He had sat there next to me for a good forty-five minutes hanging on my every word without making any familiar moves. I decided to take the bull by the horns. "Look," I said huskily, "I don't know what your deal is, but I need to tell you right now, I'm gay and I'm really attracted to you." He nodded and moved in a little closer. "That's cool," he said. "You want to go out sometime? Maybe catch a movie?" He smiled encouragingly.

"Sure," I said. "I'll give you a call then," he said. "Great," I replied. He hesitated for a few seconds and then he hugged me hard and let me go quick. "Later on," he said and was out my door and gone, his soft, barefooted retreat down the wooden steps followed by the harsh roar of the Duster.

For the next week we seemed to run into each other at least once a day. From Kitty Hawk down to Whalebone Junction is a pretty big step, but it's all along two straight stretches of, then, two-lane road. No matter where I found myself along the beach road or the bypass, I met Rick coming or going. On Wednesday of the next week I was filling up my car at the 7-Eleven on the bypass near Joe's. Rick and I saw each other as he passed by. He did a U-turn between traffic and pulled up beside me.

"I've been thinking about me and you . . . about . . . you know," he said over the car's low growl. I said, "Yeah, me too," as I hung up the gas nozzle. "So, you still want to, maybe, I don't know, go out Friday night? Maybe check out a movie or something," he said. I was all, like, nervous and shit. It was as if I'd regressed from twenty-four to fourteen in one horny minute. When I could look at him, I said, "That would be really great."

We played the look–look away–look thing before he said, "I'll pick you up, like eight, eight-thirty?" I answered his smile with one of my own. "Cool," I said, feeling really shy and high all at the same time. He put his car in drive and said, "I like that." "Like what?" I asked. He just grinned and pulled away fast.

I drove over to Joe's, where I was heading in the first place. He was cooking dinner. I opened the door with my key and said, "You ain't gonna believe what just happened." Joe left the stove to give me hug and said, "Tell your daddy what happened, baby." I pulled away and found my place on the pew in the bay window. "You remember me telling you about that surfer-construction guy I met at the gym who stopped by my house?"

Joe nodded as he made his way to the refrigerator. "Well, he just asked me out Friday night." Joe rolled his eyes and asked, "You want some iced tea?" I nodded and blindly went on in my excitement. "I mean, I made it pretty clear I wanted to sleep with him." Joe set the glass of iced tea on the table in front of me and folded his arms over his chest.

"You ought to just stop. You ain't got no business fucking with that straight boy," he said. I waved him off as I lit a cigarette. "It ain't no big deal. He's probably just curious. I imagine it's going to be a hit and run, just for fun." Joe snorted as he set an ashtray down by my glass of iced tea. "He may want to hit and quit, but from the way you're talking, you're going to want to lay and stay."

"Fuck that," I said, exhaling a long stream of smoke. "I've been that bitch," I said, wondering if I was really that transparent. Joe walked over to the sink and picked up a dish rag. "You mark my words. You keep fucking with these straight men and you're going to mess yourself up one of these days, and don't say I didn't warn you."

I twirled the end of my cigarette slowly against the side of the ashtray and thought about pulling loose the snap and Velcro fly of Rick's bathing suit. "Damn, Joe. It might just be a movie and him saying he's sorry, but he really can't do it." Joe shook his head and walked back to the stove.

"What are you going to see?" He asked. I thought about it a minute. I didn't recall me or Rick ever mentioning any specific movie. "I don't know. What's playing?" I asked. Joe stirred a pot and looked back over his shoulder. He said, "Make him take you to see *Sophie's Choice*. If he still wants to fuck you after that depressing movie, you'll have all the answers you need, I guess."

I vaguely remember Meryl Streep screaming, "Take my daughter!" on the railroad tracks of Auschwitz. What is burned into my memory is the smell of Right Guard and the unrelenting pressure of Rick's bare leg pressed against mine and the feel of his toes, kneading the top of my foot ever so gently for almost three hours. It seems as if the camera's long pan over the lifeless bodies of Meryl Streep and Kevin Kline into the spring green of the trees outside their bedroom moved from the blue sky beyond to Rick and me in the hot, dark interior of the Plymouth Duster. "You want to go back to my house?" I asked. "I'd like that a lot," he said.

I put U Roy on the stereo and sat on the sofa while Rick went to the bathroom. I was nervous. Somehow, I was receiving signals that I was getting into something deeper than I ever had before. It was a baffling sort of prescience. I was certainly no virgin. I'd always had sex with the single-minded drive of a bitch in heat. Eerily, I felt the inevitable following act was somehow going to connect love with sex. I felt my foot about to hit the slippery edge.

When Rick came back into the living room, he just stood and looked at me. Finally, he said, "What are you doing way over there?" I looked up at him and thought a minute before I answered. "I really want to be with you a lot, but I ain't looking for no recruits. You know what I mean?"

Rick never broke his gaze as he pulled his T-shirt over his head and dropped it on the floor. "C'mere," he said. I stood and walked up to him. He was my height to the inch. I could feel the heat coming off him. I could smell his particular scent of clean sweat and something deeper, like patchouli under the Right Guard. "I made up my mind about me and you that first time I came over," he chuckled. Delighted, I said, "Why come you waited this damn long to let me know?"

He didn't answer; he put his hands on my hips, pulled me into his broad chest, and nuzzled his face into my neck. I moved to kiss him. He moved his head away and looked at me with a quick wariness. I looked him back in the eye and whispered, "You don't kiss. You don't fuck. I'm too good to get it halfway." As he hesitated, I looked down and moved to break away. He pulled me back and kissed me long and slow and sweet. I started falling then, and I didn't stop for eight years.

Of the next few hours and the next few months, I could say a great deal or not much. I guess I should say he fit himself into me and me into him in the first complete sexual intimacy I'd ever known. More than that, I delighted in every minute I was with him, in or out of bed.

For a long time, it was easy laughs and clouds chasing themselves in a blue sky over the dunes north of Rodanthe. It was a purplish ocean breaking high overhead before the tide turned and the sun went down behind Penny Ridge. Always and every minute the taste and feel of him lingered in my mouth and on my skin. He insinuated himself so completely into my mind and flesh, like your body still feels the movement of the sea long after you come in from the waves. Alone, I could feel him moving in me and over me, completing me.

The unfortunate truth was that it wasn't enough for Rick. It was only partly right, and in his return to older urges, it stopped being right for me. Too soon a girlfriend entered the picture. I knew and I didn't want to know. I'd already given up three hundred bucks in dribbles and drabs, willfully not listening to the rumors that the money had bought Rick a way out of a little problem growing with his face on it.

Joe never said, "I told you so." I give him credit for that. At first, I think he didn't dislike Rick so much as he disliked the stark lines I drew separating the two of them. I think he did come to dislike him in the growing disgust he was feeling for me. Blind to the inevitable and addicted to a long line of lies in the night, my emotional equilibrium started to wobble. That internal gyroscope of reason stuttered in desperate arcs and finally fell.

One night just before Christmas, Joe called and asked me to go eat pizza with him. It had been a while since we had spent any time together, I'd been so wrapped up in Rick. He even offered to pick me up.

That night, I was by myself and had been for a few days. Though Rick had a key and we'd been practically living together for months, more and more he was showing up sporadically, if at all. He was going days without calling and then showing up all loving like nothing was going on. He always had some bullshit excuse and a sincerely hard dick. However, the beach wasn't that big and I wasn't blind or deaf. Finally, my pride was on the line. I told him if he kept on fucking with me, I would get to a point where I didn't care what it made me look like, I'd get my get-backs. Rick didn't listen. He knew he had a hold on me right where my pride ended, and it was a lot lower than my heart.

I knew the girl he was fucking. She had been a neighbor of mine a couple of years before when she stayed on Highview Street a ways down from my house. Her mama was three hundred pounds of white trash who had this girl by some sorry piece of shit who'd run off on her. Somewhat lighter, but no less discerning, she got her son by a carnival worker. Ostensibly born again, she and her young'uns lived off welfare and the charity of the fundamentalist, charismatic Rock Church.

I had my suspicions. I just needed some proof on Rick's I'm-such-a-stud-I'm-so-slick ass. I told Joe, "Hell, yeah. Come on up and get me. I'm hungry." We went to Pizza Hut and I half listened to what was up with Joe through my own preoccupation with calling Rick on his bullshit. Leaving the restaurant, I hit on an idea.

Back in the car on the way home, I asked Joe to turn on a back road off the bypass. He asked me, "What do you want to go back up in there for?" I shrugged and asked him if he wanted to do it or not. He said, "I ain't going to help you hunt your stupid boyfriend." I just said, "Turn here."

White-knuckled but silent, he did. I directed him through two more turns on dark roads until the headlights hit Rick's Duster head on. Rick and the little girl were slung up necking in the front seat. Blocked, Joe stopped his car, and Rick looked up blindly into the headlights' glare as the girl hid her face.

"All right. Let's go," I said. Without a word, Joe backed up and drove us in silence back to my house. I thanked him for supper and he said furiously, "I cannot believe you used me to do that to yourself." Actually, I felt a deep calm I hadn't felt for a long time. "Do what to myself?" I asked. "You know perfectly well what I mean. I know you're not as dumb as you want to make yourself out to be. Not as innocent either," Joe said in controlled fury.

I fumbled for my cigarettes and lit one up. "Stupid little cunt," I said, as I cracked the window and flicked out the match. "Who are you calling a stupid little cunt? It looks to me like you're just as bad, if not worse," he said. I didn't say anything, I just opened the door. "You know I don't like you very much right now," Joe said. I bent down and looked back at him in the car. "Yeah? Well, you're in good company then, 'cause I ain't real happy with myself either," I said, as I closed the door. I heard Joe yell, "Don't you go and do anything stupid!" as I went up the steps.

I got in the house and poured myself a long drink of vodka and didn't even pretend to put any orange juice in it. I sat in the dim light from the window by the kitchen table and let the tiny and thorough grinding of my mind turn. Greased by vodka and nicotine, I had it all figured out by the time the Duster choked out under the house and Rick's key turned in the lock.

"Hey," I said throatily from the dark. Rick jerked a little, but recovered quickly. "What're you doing sitting by yourself in the dark?" he asked as he kicked off his sneakers. "Just drinking and thinking," I said gently. "What are you thinking about?" he asked as he came up beside me. "Just stuff," I said.

Rick moved away and emptied his pockets on the bar. I watched him undress and toss his clothes on the sofa. He scratched his chest and moved toward me. In the dimness, I could see his half-hard dick swing out heavily. He said, "You miss me?" I could smell the cheap Avon perfume in the chilly room. I reached out and traced the tips of my fingers down his hip between the beginning and ending of his tan lines.

"Yeah, I missed you," I said. "Are you pissed off?" he asked, as he gently put his hand on the side of my face and pulled my head into his side. "You know I always come home." He lifted my face by my chin to look up at him. Stroking my cheek with his thumb, he said, "Let's go to bed." He let me go, turned, and walked toward the bedroom in the dark, confident I would follow. It was a good thing he couldn't see my eyes. He always told me they were beer colored. Right then, I figured they were glowing yellow as a cat's.

The next day at work I picked as much information as I could from a lady at work who went to Rock Church. She couldn't conceal her delight and triumph in the fact that Rick was once again walking down the right side of the street. With a great deal of condescending empathy for me, she told me all about how he had been coming to church with his new girlfriend.

I shook my head pitifully and limped away from her self-righteous gloat. She didn't know I was limping from the proper pounding Rick had given me the night before and again just that morning. The result of all that necking had to go somewhere; it came home to me. I was the surprise winner because I knew how these born-again, white-trash chicks played the game. They keep the guy horny for weeks until he's got enough cum backed up that when they do give it up, they get pregnant right off the bat. Boom, their hand shows a baby and a sure-thing bet on winning a husband from the guy with his dick on the table and his nuts about to go in the pot to see the bet she raises. Obviously, Rick's little girlfriend had been taking lessons from her mama, even though that fat sow had gone bust more than once. There's only one game white trash knows how to play.

Unfortunately, none of them counted on me coming to the table. Like any good gambler, I knew how to force the hand. Rick might not be all mine, but he wasn't going to be any of hers. In fact, if he didn't play his hand just right, he might end up with none of me either. There were some things going on that he didn't know about. I was getting an opportunity to make a clean break that I kept to myself.

That night, I went and got myself a Lab puppy. I named him Tank and figured he'd be company if things didn't go as planned. The next day, I heard from the Rock Church lady at work that Rick and his girlfriend had been at church the night before.

Rick kept a room back on Colington Island at the house of a guy he worked with. This guy's girlfriend was Rick's girlfriend's best friend. That's how they met. At lunch, I went over there. Rick's car was in the yard. He had skipped work. I let myself in the house and found my way back to his room. He was still asleep on the mattress on the floor. There was a used rubber beside the bed. Disgusted, I was glad he at least had enough sense to use one after his direct hit a few months back.

I kicked him in the ribs and said, "Wake up, you stupid fuck." He groaned and rolled over and put the pillow over his head. I grabbed an empty beer bottle off the dresser and threw it against the wall over his head. That got his attention. He sat up and said, "Damn. You ain't playing are you?"

I smiled. "Me and you are going to have a little talk. When we finish, you're going to make some decisions." He groaned and fell back on his pillow. I picked up another empty. "Fuck," he said. "All fucking right. I'll get up."

I started talking as he pulled on a pair of jeans, following him outside to the deck. Calmly, I laid it all out for him as I saw it. I told him essentially that he had to pick. It was her or me. Not both. I told him to think before he said anything. He motioned for a cigarette and I gave him one and took one myself. He fished a lighter out of his back pocket and lit them both. We smoked in silence in the chilly air. It was getting colder by the minute.

Finally, he looked at me and said, "You can't understand. It's impossible for you. I'm not gay. A real man's got to do what a man's got to do." I looked at him with a fury that made me stone-cold sober and calm. "Is that your answer?" I asked him. He flicked away the butt of his cigarette and stood threateningly, inches from my face. He said, "I suppose it has to be." I flicked my cigarette out toward his. "I guess I understand that good enough," I said, and walked away.

On Christmas Eve, an Alberta Clipper blew down the East Coast with the coldest winds our beach had ever recorded, bringing with it a lonesome howl. Joe had gone to Suffolk to be with his family. I hadn't seen or heard from Rick since we had our little talk at his place on Colington. Christmas morning, I took my puppy and drove to Avalon Pier to check out the waves. A wave broke over the bulkhead and splashed the windshield of my car. The seawater froze before the wipers could sweep it away. It was pretty grim, but it matched how I was feeling inside.

I headed home and thawed out some ice cubes to make coffee, as my pipes had frozen. Fortunately, the electricity was still on. I turned on the radio. WOWI had the "Soulful Sounds of the Season" playing. I turned on the lights of the spindly cypress tree I'd cut down out of the scrub across from my office; it was decorated with some old ornaments Joe had lent me. They sparkled desperately against the grayness outside the window.

I heard the Duster before I saw it turn under the house. My puppy began to bark excitedly and ran to greet Rick at the kitchen door. He let himself in with stamping feet and steaming breath. "Hey, little guy," he said as he squatted down to roughhouse with the puppy. He looked up at me from the puppy's yapping and said, "Merry Christmas." I felt the tear inside me rip a little farther down. "Merry Christmas," I said, and offered him the last of the coffee.

He refused, saying he was on his way somewhere else and he didn't want to bother me. "When did you get the dog?" He asked. "It's been awhile. I don't remember," I said as I moved to pour myself a cup of coffee. He fished inside his jacket and pulled out two small, inexpertly wrapped gifts. Placing them on the bar, he said "I got these for you before. . . . Anyway, I'd still really like you to have them."

I smiled and said, "Yours are under the tree." He grinned and tugged at my arm as he sprinted excitedly by me to sprawl on the floor and rip open the boxes. I didn't move. He peeled off his jacket, letting it fall to the floor where he sat, and pulled a brand-new sweater out of the box and over his head.

From the floor he looked up at me with sadness and love. "It fits me like a hug," he said sincerely. I smiled and turned away to hide the riot that was going on in my eyes. I busied myself stirring my coffee. I felt him behind me. I turned and he handed me a present that rattled thinly under the cheerful wrapping. "Open this one first," he said.

I tore tentatively at the flimsy package and found a thick, silver, serpentine chain wrapped around the pretty front of a Christmas card. The greeting panel had been carefully torn away. Loosening the chain from the cardboard, it slipped softly into the gaps between my fingers as I stared down at it.

"Can I put it on?" Rick asked gently. I just looked up at him. "C'mere," he said as he took the chain from my fingers. Opening the clasp, he flipped the chain over the back of my head and brought the two ends together, working at the small catch with the blunt ends of his thick fingers until he got it hooked. He gently guided the clasp to the back of my neck and held me by my shoulders at arm's length.

"I like that," he said. I thanked him, and he started to pull me toward him. "Don't," I said, more sharply than I had intended. He rubbed his thumbs into my shoulders and said, "Can I come back later? I really need to talk to you." I just looked at him. "We can work this out," he said. I looked away and nodded okay. Rick squeezed my shoulders quickly and dropped his hands.

"I'm just going to leave my presents here, okay?" he said as he took his light jacket from the puppy and pulled it on over the bulky sweater. "Sure," I said. He moved past the excited puppy toward the door. "I'll be back late, but I'll be back, I swear," he promised. I nodded. He reached over and lifted my face in one hand. "It's you. I really love you, you know that." For a second I willingly let my cheek rest in his warm palm. "Yeah, I know," I said.

He opened the door to the brutal wind. "Don't forget to open your other present," he yelled as he went down the stairs. I closed the door and rested my hot forehead against the cold pane of glass until I heard the Duster rev furiously and then fade off down the street.

I shushed the puppy and went for my coffee and cigarettes. My other present was on the bar. Opening it, I found a blue nylon wallet with a Velcro close. I ripped the flap back and opened up the wallet. Inside, the picture compartment had two pictures of Rick and me taken at Avalon Pier the summer before.

I took the wallet, my coffee, and my cigarettes over to the sofa and turned up the volume on the radio. WOWI was playing the Temptations singing "Silent Night." I looked at the pictures in the wallet and allowed myself a minute to wonder if setting these wheels in motion was the right thing to do.

The puppy was worrying a wad of wrapping paper and cardboard on the floor. I took it away from him, wondering how I'd managed to get the wrapping paper from my necklace on the floor. I hadn't. That was still on the bar. This must have fallen out of Rick's coat pocket. I carefully unwadded the paper and cardboard and smoothed them out on my thigh. The cardboard was the other half of the Christmas card Rick had given me. There was writing on the cardboard in a hand I didn't recognize. Reading it, I realized that my necklace had been a gift to Rick from his girlfriend.

I had to give him credit, not only was he smooth, but I suddenly liked the chain all the more. I shook my head, admiring how well he managed to play both ends against the middle. I stood up and walked over to the Christmas tree. I unplugged it and dragged it out onto the deck. I threw it over the railing, lights, decorations, and all. Looking at its pitiful abandonment in the cold sand, my resolve hardened. I went back inside. Just about everything was packed already.

I went into the spare room and pulled out a large unmarked box that had all of Rick's stuff in it. I dragged it into the kitchen and set it on the bar. Very neatly, I put Rick's Christmas presents from me in the box. Then I walked over to the phone and called my buddy Chip. When he answered, I told him I was ready. He said cool, but he needed to get done and back with the truck in time to go to his wife's folks for Christmas dinner. I unplugged the phone and put it in another box in the spare room.

I had never told Rick my lease got voided by my landlords, who decided they wanted to live in the house themselves. Fortunately, this lady who owned a surf shop on the bypass nearby was splitting up with her boyfriend and business partner. They had lived together over the shop for years. Deciding she couldn't stand to live there anymore after she forced him out, she happily rented the place to me.

I didn't have a lot. That was a good thing because it started to sleet while Chip and I were in the middle of the second, and last, big load. What was left I could fit in my car without any help. He dropped me off back at my old place to get the last little bit of stuff and the puppy.

I stood in the empty rooms and remembered a lot of things. Strands of blond hair were still in the carpet from when Joe cut my hair right after Thanksgiving. All the smoking passion and sweat Rick and I spent seemed to leave a residue on the walls of the bedroom. I had forgotten to pack Rick's spare contact lens case. It was sitting on the back of the bathroom sink. I dropped it into his box on the bar. I picked up the puppy, gave Rick's box a farewell pat, turned off the lights, and left my bright spring house in the dark winter's night.

My new place out on the bypass was a bit lonesome, with only a small strip shopping center and an Amoco station for neighbors. It did have an ocean view, with only a sweeping stretch of beach scrub and grass between the generous back deck and the row of cottages along the beach. It was twice as large as my old place, and that was really nice. Heat and air were included in the rent. It was a palace by my standards. And Rick didn't have a key.

I unpacked my sparse belongings and hooked up the stereo right away. By nine that night, I was curled up on my sofa, warm and snug, with the puppy sleeping at my feet. I was drinking a huge mug of hot chocolate liberally laced with Kahlúa. It was sweet enough to make my teeth ache, but it made a nice counterpoint to the good sinse bud I'd stashed away from Rick.

By far and away, it was turning out to be a pretty good Christmas after all. Feeling more than a little smug at my clean getaway and good planning, I allowed myself to recall with relish the synchronicity of events after I'd left Rick in his nasty place on Colington Island.

Immediately after leaving the island, I swung by work and begged the afternoon off from my ever-patient, long-suffering boss. Then, I headed back to the surf shop to drop off my rent deposit in cash. Delighted, my new landlord graciously told me I could move in a week early for free.

That accomplished, I went home, walked the puppy, and went over my dialogue in my head. The phone call I was about to make would be the most demanding role I'd ever attempted in my long history of deviousness and manipulation. Calmly, I picked up the phone and called the preacher at Rock Church. Knowing just how to grab his attention and keep it, I tearfully informed him about the sad and sick little triangle between me, Rick, and his sixteen-year-old church member. I dropped enough salacious details to keep his interest and later beg his forgiveness for.

Just to twist the knife, I threw in a few personally painful things with which Rick had trusted me. I ended up asking the preacher to pray for me. He promised he'd check into the sins I'd alleged between Rick and his girlfriend and plan some counseling once he learned the true depth of their transgression. Of course, I was beyond redemption, being both Catholic and queer, but he tried his best not to gag on his earnest sympathy.

All in all, it was a good day's work. I figured I'd best get missing before Rick found out what I'd done. I knew I wouldn't be too hard to find, but I hoped it would take long enough that he'd only beat the shit out of me and not shoot my ass.

With everything seeming to fall so neatly into place, to contrive both my escape and to exact my revenge, I finished my Kahlúa and cocoa and went to bed alone in my new house that Christmas night. However, that night's smugness wasn't properly earned. I hadn't accurately gauged the depth of Rick's feelings for me or his bird-dogging abilities. Hidden as I was, in plain sight, I had counted on his reluctance to publicly come after me, one way or another.

Between Christmas and New Year's, Rick followed up his suspicions as to my whereabouts with a string of rather reckless inquiries to my co-workers, my godparents, and my neighbors. None of them liked him well enough to tell him where I was outright—some even passed along the word that he wasn't really welcome—but each told him enough to give him a scent to track.

New Year's Eve, I opened my back door to find him standing on the other side of the screen door. Just looking at him started a riot of conflict in my mind. My heart pumped a sudden release of adrenaline that triggered a fight-or-flight reaction in my mind. I didn't know if the preacher had confronted him with the revelations of my phone call or not. At the same time, I was so happy to see him I didn't care.

"Why did you move and not tell me?" he asked quietly. I looked past him toward the beach and didn't say anything. "Aren't you going to let me in?" he asked simply. I was a little taken aback by the anxiety in his voice, but I was still hurt. I said, "I don't know."

Rick shook his head and looked away before he said, "I'm not going anywhere." This was an old saying between us. We had used it in moments of intimacy and fierce celebration of finding the connection between us. Both damaged and dented by so many other things outside of what we were together, we found our separate rough edges met with the certainty of puzzle pieces. I opened the screen door, he came in, and we quickly found that fit of bodies and feelings again.

Still, for all the clean welding of hot emotions and hotter attraction, the seam couldn't hold. Within weeks, he decided to return North to live on his own with his dad. He had started painting himself into a corner long before he met me. He just finally ran out of room. When his dad offered to mend fences, he decided that starting college this late was still a better alternative to construction work.

Emotionally exhausted, I actually encouraged him to go. Somehow I knew I'd keep him loving me longer and better if I let his leash play out as far as it would go. In an odd way, as ready as I was to humiliate myself to get back at him for his two-timing, I was selfless enough to let him do what was best for him. Love is a bitch.

It ended up I was right, though it just about drove me crazy to let him walk away. Of course, he contributed to that by refusing to stay gone. Emotionally and sexually addicted to each other, we were a mess for more than a few years. Turns out my gamble paid off, but it cost me. It cost me a lot.

The preacher and the girlfriend? Well, thanks to the preacher's due diligence and the girlfriend's disingenuous revelation that Rick planned to come down from Philadelphia and take her away, that all played out about a month after Rick left.

I was sitting on my living-room floor one night, having the best night I could remember since he'd left. I'd bought the first album Yes had come out with in years, gotten stoned, and was contentedly playing with the puppy on the floor when the phone rang. I picked it up to Rick's barely controlled fury, saying, "If I was down there I'd take a shotgun and fucking kill you right now." I just took it for awhile until he boiled down to a simmer. "I told you if you kept on fucking with me, I didn't care what it made me look like, I'd take you down," I said gently. Rick was quiet for a minute and then he kind of chuckled. "Yeah, I guess you did," he said. "Aren't you glad you're not saddled with a high school dropout wife and a snot-nosed brat up there in Yankee land?" I asked. He didn't say anything. "Gets awful cold banging nails for minimum wage in the snow, baby. At least you're back in school," I said to the silence at the other end of the line.

"Yeah, you're always thinking for me, aren't you?" he said finally. "Somebody's got to; you do all your thinking with the head of your dick," I said. Rick snorted, then laughed. "So what are you doing right now?" he asked. "I got a buzz on and I'm just playing with Tank and listening to the new Yes album," I replied, knowing I was already forgiven. "You're such a fucking bitch, I don't know why I miss you so goddamn much," he said.

I didn't say anything. I just reached for my cigarettes and lit one up. The silence on the line was interrupted by distant hisses and pops. "You know I still love you," he said into the phone, his voice low, and then hung up.

After all these years, I haven't come to any single conclusion about why Rick loved me. He wasn't always the dog I make him out to be. He really did love me and gave me a part of himself he didn't give anyone else. A child of divorce, he was shuttled between his mom and dad most of his life. He got in trouble with the law, with girls, and with me. He was as big a mess as I was.

I suppose, in me, he found a compatriot and a sexual equal. I also made him a home he had never had, and no matter how badly he acted out, I stuck with him. No matter how many flaming hoops he set up for me to jump through, I never stopped loving him. Equal to all that, I think he admired the fight I had in me.

As for me, hell, there was a time I would have crawled across broken glass to get to him. When I was just a kid watching *Flipper* on TV, I'd idealized a lover. Rick was my Sandy. I would have fought the devil himself to keep him. I got to fuck him and be with him off and on for eight years. It cost me my pride, my heart, and almost my sanity, in the wake of his running in and out of my life.

We have a lot of history together. Every time we came back together we fell into each other effortlessly. At the end, Rick found me in Raleigh. We got together at the beach to see where we were. We talked, halfway seriously, of getting back together. He extended his stay to go back to Raleigh with me. He thought Raleigh was pretty cool. He had a high-tech degree by then and a ton of jobs were available. We even talked about me moving to Philadelphia.

All the talking turned to arguing. In the midst of it all, here comes Joe, some secret, protective radar alerting him I was about to go off the deep end, again. Joe showed up at my door. By then, Joe and Rick couldn't stand the sight of each other. Rick said hello and slunk off into the bedroom and closed the door. Joe and I talked, but he could tell that all my concentration was focused on the other room. Long resigned to my addiction to the man in there to the detriment of everything else, Joe stood to leave.

I walked him down to his car to say good-bye. Joe hugged me and said, "Don't let him tear you apart again, baby." I laughed and said, "No, I've been that bitch." Joe snorted and said, "Uh huh. You still are his bitch. Face it, you aren't ever going to get over him as long as you keep this shit up." I looked off and said, "It's different this time." Joe hugged me against his long frame and said, "Yeah, right. You know where I am if you need me."

The next morning I woke up wrapped in Rick's arms and legs. We were stuck together by years of spit and cum and an inexplicable gravity from which neither one of us could completely break free. I woke him up. His leaving was only a short time away. He got up and went to the bathroom. I lay under the ceiling fan feeling like someone had torn away a layer of my own skin.

Rick came back and stood in the doorway to the bedroom. He was fuller now than he had been when I first met him. He was a fully fleshed-out man. The rawboned edges had smoothed under the maturation of his muscle. The down of blond hair running from his groin to his navel was darkening and thickening. His dick hung at a heavier level in the fullness of his constant morning erection. I knew the changes in his body better than I knew those of my own.

With absolute tenderness he looked at me sprawled naked and waiting like he'd done carelessly a thousand times before. I wondered if he saw the same enduring constellations in my flesh as I saw in his. We'd navigated our way to and from each other by the brilliance of that passion one more time. Rick came back to bed and claimed what had been his for a long time.

Our bodies never schemed or lied. There was always a fundamental truth in our lovemaking. He looked for it again, his dick filling up my gut as though he was burrowing up into my heart to find himself waiting there to be told what to do next. It was all the sweeter and stronger for the years of finding and leaving and fighting and fucking that had gone before it. He finished just as I did. In synch to the end.

We got up, showered, and dressed. I had him at the airport on time. Waiting at the gate, he turned to me and said, "I love you more than I ever have. But goddamn you, I'm not gay. I'll never be there for you the way you want me to be."

I wish now I'd behaved better. I calmly told him if he ever did this to me again, I'd kill him and then myself. I just couldn't take it anymore. "If you love me, go and stay gone," I said. He nodded, gave me a quick hug and a longer, unembarrassed kiss. He walked away, hesitated, and then kept on going down the jet bridge. That was the last time I ever saw him.

That night, I went to a gay club called the Capital Corral. Joe always said there was nothing like the next one to get you over the last one. I picked up a marine just out of basic training on his first leave. I took him home and fucked him with the single-minded purpose of removing Rick's touch and taste from any part of me that horny boy could reach.

He left worn out, dazed, and grateful just before dawn the next morning. *Semper fi,* baby. Unexorcised, Rick's presence stayed in my soul. Alone, I watched the sun come up and shut off every emotion I had left, one by one.

Then, I threw some stuff in my wetsuit bag and headed home to Joe in Nags Head.

Chapter 9

Family of Choice

Twice each year, I join a huge extended family for a beach week-end. We rent out an entire 1950s-style motel on the southern tip of Singer Island, Palm Beach's poor relation to the north. The people who go each year began with a core family but extended over time to include friends and friends of friends. For years now, I have attended these biannual reunions with greater regularity than those of my kin. This is my Florida family, the one I chose or, rather, who chose me.

I was introduced to this group by my partner, Jeff, before we even began living together. In a way, they were the final litmus test I had to pass for Jeff to fully incorporate me into his life. It was easier to meet his blood family than this horde of friends who had knitted themselves into one another's lives since high school. This was to be no series of polite dinners with breaks for decompression; this was total immersion, seventy-two hours, nonstop.

Fortunately, I had little to fear. This Singer Island crew collectively extended their open arms and drew me into their sheltering warmth without reservation. Unconditional acceptance is a rare gift, especially after they've heard you sing "Sitting on the Dock of the Bay" after four margaritas and a half pack of cigarettes. That is family of choice.

Of course, this is the broadest example of a concept that no one defined as such before our lives became splintered from the immediate environment of blood kin. The past fifty-odd years of American history have produced an overwhelming variety of stimuli for social migration among white and middle-class populations. Religious, ethnic, and class-oriented communities had been scattered by economic, educational, and social opportunities on an unprecedented scale before that time, but these migrations' effects weren't legitimized, analyzed, and given a trendy moniker until the white folks started doing it.

Certainly, there was a great black migration from the closed, rural society of the South to the promise of Northern jobs and personal freedoms before World War II. Gay people, as a group, have migrated to cities in search of community throughout the nation's urban history. With the sum total of this diaspora, close social networks of kinship reinforced by proximity mutated to ones based on personal freedom of choice heretofore unknown in the social fabric.

In the second half of this century, it became a reality that an individual could, indeed, choose his or her closest relationships based on a specifically defined set of personal preferences, as op-posed to taking what one could get from the family to which one was born. Removed far from the restraints and comforts of family, intimate friendships became as important, if not more so.

The family of choice is engraved in gay literature as the most enduring of all adult relationships. If you read the excellent work of Andrew Holleran, you will find individual characters who retain their identities or become easily recognized composites that run like a common thread through each book or short story. Sutherland of *Dancer from the Dance* becomes Mister Friel of *Nights in Aruba* and later short stories.

Either as Sutherland or Mister Friel, this character remains the touchstone of continuity for the lead character or the narrator. In-credibly intelligent, socially glib, and privately profound, this char-acter is indeed the mentor of all gay immigrants to Manhattan in the 1970s. One marvels at the importance of the individual (or individ-uals) who inspired Holleran to create such a family figure for his protagonists. It is a given of gay life. A Sutherland is absolutely essential for any gay man's integration into the larger gay world. His closest friends are the closest and most reliable family to pro-vide support and succor.

What makes fiction successful is its representation of common experience in an objectifiable form. Certainly for me, I can see the faces of the closest members of my extended family that I have created for myself in the mirror of fiction. It is not difficult to recognize a form of what Joe Riddick represents in my life in gay literature. What is more amazing is the interconnectedness of gay friendships that result from that one source.

I asked Joe bluntly whom he considered his family of choice. He replied with five names. Of the five, my partner Jeff and I counted as two. Of the remaining three, I shared only one name. That was Trent Lewis. When I name my family of choice, he figures prominently as well. When I think of the ripples of friendship that radiate from his centrality, he becomes more important still.

Individually, Trent represents the degree to which I have been knitted into Joe's life. Joe and Trent were lovers briefly in the early 1970s. After the passion and following melodrama played themselves out, Joe and Trent took another look at each other and found an empathy that has endured for almost thirty years. Through other lovers and good and bad times, they have sustained a conversation that is the repository of history for each other's lives.

When I first met Trent, he had a boyfriend of some years' duration. They had driven to Nags Head for a weekend visit the summer Joe took me to raise. On Saturday night, we all went to party in Norfolk. On the trip up, I became enchanted with Trent's easy monologue and co-narration of the events of Joe's life.

Providing a badly needed counterpoint to Joe's encyclopedic collection of gay lore and personal experience, Trent's humor was a dry delight. As the years went by and I became a part of their history, Trent graciously adopted me into the closest circle of the family he and Joe had created together. In my years on and off the beach, Trent and I have sustained our own relationship with each other. Like Joe, he has seen my ups and downs and has stuck by me through some extremes of each. Beyond that, Trent is just good company.

A few years after Trent and I met found us at opposite geographic points of a triangle with Joe. Each of us living in separate cities, we still managed to get together every few months. On Joe's birthday one year, I left home to collect Trent on our way to Suffolk, where Joe had retreated from the beach. We had a pleasant drive together, just Trent and I, catching up and gently dissecting Joe and each other.

Arriving at Joe's front door, we were greeted by a short, muscular guy whom Joe introduced as Brad. This Brad froze like a deer caught in headlights on our unexpected arrival and bolted almost immediately. Sharing hugs and shedding our coats, Trent asked, "Who was that person who was almost here?" Joe shrugged and said, "Just some squid I picked up last night at the Garage, and, child, he like to wore me out."

Trent and I laughed and prodded him for gory details as he made us coffee. Nothing is sacred to the two people who knew you when and know you now. I recall saying, "I think he was cute. I didn't really get a good look at him. Are you going to see him again?" Joe was noncommittal. "I doubt it. He's shipping out on a Mediterranean cruise on an aircraft carrier in a few days."

Trent asked what he did on the aircraft carrier and Joe idly waved him off, "Who knows? Whatever these children do on a ship that big." Trent harrumphed and asked gently, "Just how old is this boy?" Joe reached for the coffee pot and said, "Too young for me."

We all laughed and moved on to other things, falling as we did into laughter and the ease of friends who fit one another like an old pair of blue jeans. Brad, however, was not so easily dismissed. His Med cruise offered plenty of time for correspondence. He wrote Joe long letters to which Joe responded with increasing interest. When Brad came back, he and Joe went out again. They've been together now for eleven years.

Brad admits to some difficulty in adjusting to the infrequent bursts of intimacy brought on by visits from Trent and me. Still living many miles apart when Joe and Brad set up housekeeping, Trent and I made regular appearances like a carnival sprung on their quiet lives. We'd arrive on a Friday evening or early Saturday morning, claiming drinks first and undivided attention second.

For the first few years, Brad was gracious about listening to our old stories over and over. Some of them, I'm sure he would have rather not heard. No one likes to hear of the prior sexual exploits of one's lover. Also, there is the admittedly experiential component to stories that brings gales of laughter to the participants and only a puzzled look from the audience.

Despite the very real feelings of having crashed a party that had been going on for years, Brad persevered. With time, he became as much a part of the stories told and retold as any of us. Indeed, he brought his own stories to the table. For Trent and me, he passed a more strenuous probation period than he probably had with Joe. He rightfully earned his place in our collective life together.

Not every other suitor was as lucky. Our oldest friends tend to be less generous in their assessments of our boyfriends. Polite at all costs, a perceptible chill comes with the introduction of any new attachment. After all, as Joe, Trent, and I have an unspoken, but practiced, commitment to one another, any new person has the right to claim a place near the center of the ripples on that pond. How long a person keeps that place is as much a matter of perseverance as it is how well that person treats his or her sponsor. The scrutiny that goes along with that place can be intimidating.

Trent and his boyfriend split up early in my tenure as a family member. From that time until the present, Trent has segregated his erotic attachments from the family. Having made the personal decision to remain single, he never really wanted to introduce the temporary attachments to the permanent fixtures. Such is his right. Even for a core group so close to one another, there is a respect for privacy and personal preferences.

There have been times when Joe and I both excluded our lovers from our chosen family. At precisely the same time I met and fell in love with Rick, Joe met and became involved with a guy named Jack. Although I loved Rick and my family of Trent and Joe, I knew I loved them each for the things that made them utterly incompatible. Of course, as my relationship with Rick became more clearly obsessive over the years, Joe and Trent wanted nothing to do with the person who obviously was driving me crazy.

Jack, on the other hand, was immediately presentable. On his introduction, I was so involved with Rick that I barely cared whom Joe was dating, as long as he was happy. Trent was more studied in his approval. For all appearances, Jack was a good match for Joe. He was good-looking, employed, and intelligent. Moreover, he was a gay fledgling who needed some direction and oversight.

Some weeks after Jack moved in with Joe, Trent came to the beach for a visit. When an opportunity for the two of us to be alone together presented itself, Trent asked me what I thought of Jack. Rarely anything but self-absorbed, I told Trent that he seemed nice enough. Joe seemed happy.

Trent took a sip of his gin and tonic and said, "There's something about that boy I just don't trust." I thought about it a minute. Jack did seem to have sort of an oily quality about him. In the generosity spawned by my own relationship, I dismissed the impression as being unfair.

"Have you said anything to Joe about this?" I asked Trent. He shook his head. "No, I haven't. Joe does seem rather happy and I don't want to spoil it for him," Trent admitted. "It has been a long while since Joe has seen anybody . . ." he continued reluctantly. He left that observation hanging.

"Well, I certainly don't want to see him hurt," I said. "But Joe's a big boy. He can look after himself." Trent concentrated on his cocktail and said, "I just don't know . . ."

As it turned out, Trent's reservations about Jack were justified. He turned out to be a con artist and a complete jerk. Fortunately, Joe saw it all coming and protected himself against any excessive emotional damage. With me and Trent, he admitted he should have known a lot sooner that Jack was a user. Even more, Joe communicated to us the deep disappointment he felt more than anything else. Jack was an example of too many of the things that made gay life so disappointingly predictable at a certain point in Joe's experience.

Collectively, Trent and I decided that on the subject of Jack, the less said, the better. There is, after all, a certain latitude you give the people you love the most to hurt themselves or others. It is precisely at that point that you discover the real meaning of loyalty, and the deep well of patience within you from which you can draw.

Halloween of the second year of my relationship with Rick found us living in two different states. Lonesome, I went to an oyster roast at Joe's house. The usual year-round crowd was there, with the addition of a cute new arrival. Dressed incongruously in a bow tie and sports coat, Mike, as he was introduced to me, had just opened his own shop on Roanoke Island.

I looked him over. Dark-haired and fresh-faced, he lit up when I asked him what kind of shop it was. He proudly explained it was an antique shop. In a gush of information, he went on to say that he had just graduated from Wake Forest University and that his dad and stepmother lived on the beach. I couldn't have cared less. I had caught the eye of Eddie, a particularly disreputable acquaintance of mine and Joe's. Eddie was just the guy I wanted to see. He was always good for a buzz.

I said something to Mike along the lines of, "Yeah, right, catch you later," before I slunk over to Eddie and asked what he had for the head. Eddie gave my ass a companionable squeeze while looking around for his lover. Seeing him, he waved him over, and the three of us took off into the house. As if on cue, the other dopers in the crowd broke away from their conversations and followed us up into Joe's loft.

Bullshitting, about six of us sat on the floor while Eddie loaded and passed around his travel bong. It had gone around the circuit a couple of times when Mike made his way up to the loft. He sat down across from me with a shy smile, which I barely acknowledged. Shortly, the bong made its way to him. He held it tentatively and said, "I've never really smoked pot before."

One of the sweetest things in the world to a room full of dopers is a virgin head. Mike presented a particularly attractive treat. Here he sat, a new boy, dressed in a navy blue blazer and a fucking bow tie. Seated at the apogee of an orbit of stoned thugs, he looked at me and said, "Could you show me how to do this?" I never said I was a nice guy.

"Sure," I said. "But you have to come over here; I'm too fucked up to move right now." Eagerly, Mike made his way over to sit by me. I took the bong from him, showed him how to put his thumb over the carburetor and how to light the bowl with his mouth over the top. I took a little baby hit to demonstrate. After mutely showing him how long to hold it in his lungs, I blew out the smoke and handed him the bong.

Silence fell as the initiate took up the sacrament. At the hiss of the lighter, everybody chanted, "Go. Go. Go. GO." I pulled the guy's thumb off the carburetor when I saw the hit shrivel. Wide-eyed and tearful, Mike tried his best to hold the smoke as long as he could. But he sort of exploded. Everybody clapped and encouraged him as he almost retched. Mike looked at me like a trusting child I'd just convinced to jump into the deep end of the pool out of sheer meanness. I patted his back and told him he did good.

Throughout the rest of the evening, he followed me around. I was so stoned and having such a good night that I was only half aware he was there, just behind my elbow. I figured it out when he followed me to my truck. Doe-eyed and earnest, he asked me where I lived. Then he asked me if I wanted some company.

I looked at him. He was cute, but he wasn't really the kind of guy I was attracted to, physically or socially. Obviously, he didn't feel the same way about me. Here was this young guy, his first winter on the beach. I felt as if a puppy was trying to follow me home. It was late. I was high. I figured, what the hell.

Now, all these years later, Mike likes to tell people I taught him how to smoke pot and how to fuck. What I don't like to tell people is how badly I treated him in the process. I knew what I represented to him. Mike really got off on my surfer-druggie-thug persona. To him, I was every menacing juvenile delinquent he was so hot for since high school. I had no plans to make any emotional investment in him, so I just played that part. Mike was just a diversion for me. I made no bones about my loyalties. I dropped him quick whenever Rick suddenly appeared.

Trent had known Mike since he was a little kid and liked him a lot. Joe thought he was a great guy. Both of them thought I treated him like shit and didn't mind telling me that in some subtle and not so subtle ways. It is a real testament to their patience with me when I told them baldly that Mike was just a transitional object for me and I was just a learning experience for him.

Despite my bad behavior, Trent and Joe gave me the run of my leash. They never cut me up behind my back when Mike asked them why I was such a coldhearted bastard. They left that up to me. Like any good family, they didn't fight my battles for me, but they didn't stab me in the back either.

Eventually, Mike resigned himself to the fact that he would always be somewhere far behind Rick in priority. He also had the incredible self-assurance to actively work at keeping my friendship, despite what had to have been an unnecessarily painful experience with me. To this day, he remains a sort of dear cousin in our family of choice. His continued friendship is something I am gifted with, never having done much to earn it. So is Trent and Joe's patience after the many times I've tested it.

Remarkably, my immediate family of choice directly mirrors my blood family in some very real ways. As Trent is the eldest and most lovingly detached of the three of us, he is much like my own father. I know he loves me even if he isn't next to me to show it. As Joe is the one who works most actively to provide both Trent and me with a sense of continuity and home, he is most like my mother. And in the experience of both sets of parents, I am the problem child who finally grew up.

Personal growth is not entirely personal. There is the nurture of the family of blood and the family of choice, and also the spur of relentless self-pruning and the dark winters of emotional neglect that allow for rest and respite. For me, growing up required those things, but I never realized any true adulthood until I came in contact with the constant sunshine of Jeff Auchter.

We met at a time when I was physically damaged by a congruence of events that began with my car being stolen, and ended with me being hit by a hit-and-run driver while riding my bike to work. I was broken in body, spirit, and bank account when a friend urged me to interview for a job with an advertising agency in South Miami. Jeff was to be my supervisor, so we talked during my interview process. He thought I was an arrogant jerk. Fortunately, the boss didn't. She hired me.

After the interview, I left the office and sat on the sidewalk with my feet in the gutter, waiting for the cab that would take me home. I didn't know it, but Jeff came outside just then to get a spare pack of cigarettes from his car. Despite my cockiness in the interview (born as it was from desperation), he saw my skinny self, arm in a cast, waiting in the gutter for a ride, and found the image touching instead of pathetic.

Over the next few weeks, separately, we withstood Hurricane Andrew. I underwent bone graft surgery and Jeff underwent an intense self-questioning regarding exactly who he was and what he wanted. The best thing that ever happened to me was his soul's answering that he was gay and he wanted me. In accepting the warmth of love and Jeff as love's source, I grew up.

On our first anniversary of living together, I dragged Jeff home for a week to see the relatives in their native habitat. He had met my mother and father when they visited us for Christmas, but that was on his own turf. I was anxious to show him my world when I was still a "me" and not a "we."

We flew into Raleigh and were met by my brother and sister-in-law. We were feted by some old friends of mine in the capital before we made our way to the Bogue Banks where Mom and Dad live. There, Jeff met some aunts and uncles who were definitely true to their natures. My beloved Uncle Johnny was immediately warm, accepting, and generous. The rest of the reactions went down the scale from polite reservation to conspicuous absence.

Finally, we made our way back to Raleigh, and Joe drove down from Suffolk to collect us. It was the first time Joe and Jeff ever met. I was not exactly apprehensive about either of their reactions. My happiness was as easy to read as a billboard. I was concerned that poor Jeff was experiencing an overload of people and travel. I also wanted Joe to know how I'd finally gotten it right.

On the drive north from Raleigh to Suffolk, I could sense Jeff relaxing in the backseat. After having been literally on display for days, Joe had immediately created an environment in which Jeff could begin to relax.

That night, we were all collected on Joe's side porch. The people who were most dear to me were all assembled in one spot: Joe in his rocker, Brad making sure everyone was comfortable and had a full glass, Trent by me on the wicker settee, and Jeff across from me, smiling and talking without reservation. There are only a few times like that one in anyone's life. It is a breath of satisfaction between ages. It is a moment of unexpected perfection before time resumes its insistent lapidary of our lives.

With the heavy Tidewater evening air settling down on us, lightning bugs putting on their show, cicadas singing their piercing, poignant poetry, the stories began. Slowly, my family of choice reached out to knit Jeff into our history. Each of us built on the last's tales of humor, lasciviousness, sorrow, meanness, and merriment.

Ending a rather long story of some Norfolk night escapade that saw Joe and me at our drugged disco worst, Joe said, "We were—" "Sluts," Brad cut in appropriately. We all laughed and the talk turned to other things. Sympathetic to Jeff's feelings, Brad hinted gracefully that it was time to return to the more important present.

Before we left to fly home, each member of this family took me aside and told me how much he liked Jeff. Each, knowing my past and my past nature better than my own pride would allow me to, warned me not to fuck this one up. Independent of one another, Joe, Brad, and Trent all said Jeff was the best thing that ever happened to me.

Flying home, Jeff told me how much he enjoyed the trip, despite its multiple locations and family members to visit and meet. It had been an exhausting string of days. "It helped me to meet the people who looked after you before I showed up. Especially Joe and Brad and Trent. Those guys were the best thing that ever happened to you," he said.

I felt the thrust of the jet engines pushing me over the ocean that connected the opposite ends of what home is to me and decided they were all right. At some point in time, I had been securely held aloft and borne home by each of them. Individually and collectively, Jeff, Joe, Brad, and Trent are the best things that ever happened to me. They are the family I chose and, more important, the family that chose me.

Chapter 10

Tests and Trials

Over the past few months, Jeff has become addicted to the History Channel. In its seemingly endless dissection of the events surrounding World War II, I have come to call it the Nazi Channel. Likewise, I have developed my own fascination with VH1's series tracking the rise and fall of certain 1970s rock icons. Jeff calls it the Rehab Channel. In both instances, the steps of the subjects' destruction seem so glaringly obvious in hindsight.

We know that if Hitler hadn't invaded Russia when he did, we might all be currently speaking German. We also know that if Fleetwood Mac hadn't been inspired by operatic romantic upheavals, *Rumours* might just be another selection in the cutout bin. The accumulation of so much happenstance and destruction parallels the etiology of illness in our own little lives. After all, what is illness but disease among nations, cultural icons, or insignificant individuals?

There is no reasoning or rationalization behind the appearance of a plague in a single population. Empirically, we can reasonably trace its movements from the activity of a certain trapper in Africa who was bitten by a monkey before flying to Amsterdam to have sex with a flight attendant on his way to a shared house on Fire Island. Where is the disease in that? With a tabloid paranoia we can perceive the decimation of an entire population as a sort of engineered social cleansing, thus proof of the disease of an entire world. The conjecture for a philosophical or moral cause and rationalization of effect rings hollowly in the echoing emptiness of the toll taken, presumably, by one casual fuck.

Could a single animal act of shared pleasure inspire massive social change? If so, then inspiration at what cost? Ask Elie Weisel. Ask Larry Kramer. Ask Joe. Ask me. There is no answer. Any effort is just a cenotaph. What remains is only an unutterable respect for the slain and, in the bewilderment of survival, a soon-forgotten obligation to the dead.

I asked Joe whether he ever wondered why he was spared. His response was immediate and final. "I never ask myself that question," he said coldly. I have not earned that decisiveness. Joe has fought against HIV on the front lines for thirteen years. He has embraced the emptiness to find his own peace with the issue. I have not.

Like a stubborn child asking repeatedly why, why, why, I look for a personal answer in the now, when it will come only much later. One day the answer may be assembled from individual lives revealed in the grainy celluloid of newsreels and the haunting testament of music.

Until then, we walk in the ruins of the culture of our past. We stumble in the craters, ripped from our collective dreams, and we do what human beings do. We willfully blind ourselves to communal pain by focusing on the disease of our own lives. It is unbearable knowing we are only people in history, ignoring the end of a time.

Looking back now, I think the end of both my and Joe's ancien régime began with the death of Joe's dad. Like a much-loved, benevolent autocrat, one could never imagine him not there, indestructible, pointing the way, making everything okay. But he died. The day inexplicably darkened to deep night in the middle of a bright, long afternoon. In the following dawn, everything was different and everything was the same.

In Old Southern culture distinct steps of mourning follow the death of a patriarch. The wake and funeral are public affairs, but the following machinations must be observed to consolidate the private power of the matriarch and install her as the *regina regnate.* Having symbolically cleaned the closets of the clothes of the dead, her next order of business is to implement her version of the will of the decedent.

Joe's dad was a successful man. He reared successful children to whom he bequeathed a means to earn a living and care for their mother. The design business his mother had started fell to Joe. That inheritance was more burden than prize. Joe had grown beyond that yoke as an individual. For Joe, his father's death presented an opportunity to leave the beach and become someone altogether new. Of course, personal needs and desires are a direct challenge to the ascendant mother.

Joe caved in. He stayed on, subordinate to the dictates of siblings and the authority of the mother-god-queen. With his future decided for him, he began to settle into its predictable course. He built himself a house. He brought home Smuthead, the store's stray cat, to care for. He dutifully got on with his life as others saw fit, even though it cast him as a tame eccentric at the manageable periphery of his family's lives.

Joe senior's death preceded my brother's by just a few months. Unlike Joe's father's passing, my brother's death was expected after being denied and hoped and prayed against for some time. Inevitably, we learned even the strongest hearts stop and cancer casually consumes lionhearted courage. Stumbling, our world righted itself, and Joe and I tried desperately to do what everyone thought we should do next.

The seeds of much disease were strewn in the wake of those two deaths. A curious complacency on Joe's part concealed a growing resentment against the object of the abrogation of his right to self-determination. Stealthily, his business began to sicken. As for me, the ground I walked on, I never really trusted. Too many times in my life it had shifted and swallowed me in darkness. I felt the first rumblings of the next great shift under my feet.

Still in the first act of my melodrama with Rick, my brother died. Then, within four weeks, my grandmother slipped away and, with her, my last refuge in the past. In the years before those events, I had become very skillful at turning off my emotions to ward off the attack of my own personal demons. I began to exercise those skills once more as I started another long slide.

Depression, for some people, is a reduction of feeling. For me, it was a complete disassociation from any feeling in the presence of unbearable pain. After successfully shutting down my feelings, I could embrace the black dogs of darkness as they ripped me with greater viciousness. I could listen as the noise collected in shrieks and whispers and dirty, gleaming insinuations in my mind. Free from normal human constraints, I stopped sleeping, I stopped eating. I was completely enthralled with the simultaneous arguments in my head and feeding the black dogs with my heart.

I've always been a high-functioning mentally ill person. It's always been a matter of pride to me to be able to walk in the world with war in my head. Like the Spartan boy, I was disciplined enough not to cry as the wolf hidden in my coat gnawed its way into my heart. Ever since I was ten years old, I knew what the consequences and rewards were for stepping too far out of line. For giving in. For letting go. For trusting anyone with the reality of exactly what lived in me.

Camouflaged larceny is practiced by the mental health worker, therapist, psychologist, and psychiatrist. They can so successfully steal the pain that sometimes is the only thing you are. Lost to that, what is there to be? They dangle the reward of the drugs. They tempt with lithium that lulls in the Librium-Atarax-Xanax-Elavil-Stelazine-Haldol-Asendin slow-rocking sea. God, how sweet the numbness is that comes in bottles when all your own efforts to achieve that kind of peace turn into hungry black dogs that shriek and growl while they eat you from the inside out. Knowing psychology's tricks, I also knew how easy it was to get the drugs and still hide and cherish the harsh and private beauty of the black dogs' ravening.

I did okay for awhile. I kept all the balls in the air. I went to work. I socialized. I laughed and cried appropriately. I had a stable affect. Then, I woke up in a Kmart parking lot somewhere outside Richmond. I had on just a bathing suit. I had my dog, Tank, with me. We were in my truck. And I had absolutely no idea how I got there. I panhandled to get some money to buy gas and went home.

At my boss's urging and Joe's insistence, I got back into the mental health dance. I wasn't a kid anymore. Everybody said I couldn't indulge the black dogs' hunger or stay spellbound by the music of chaos in my head. At the mental health clinic, I underwent a ten-minute evaluation by the circuit psychiatrist, who wrote me a script for a staggering dose of Elavil, assigned me to a therapist aide for weekly sessions, and split.

That probably would have been okay if I hadn't augmented the Elavil with my usual intake of pot for the next few months. Things did settle back into a routine. Joe put me to work on the weekends, helping him with furniture deliveries and installations. Drugged to the point where I'd stumble on a pattern in the rug, I was still a nasty little piece of work. Although I cursed out the occasional client and made fun of a few more for their bourgeoisie pretentiousness, Joe stuck with me.

It was a good thing. I was dead broke and needed the money. I also needed watching. The Elavil did little but centralize the black dogs' appetites. The pot kept the volume down on the music of the separate, horrible, taunting snarling in my head. Still, it didn't go away. I met weekly with my therapist chick, but I had been end-running psychologists for years. I cha-chaed when they wanted and waltzed beautifully on cue.

I ended up in another full-blown manic episode one fine weekend in June. Rick had appeared for awhile to store up on whatever emotional and physical needs I fed before he took off again. In the echoing emptiness he left behind, I expanded with an overflowing of staggering creativity. I was suddenly transcendent in my solitude.

I threw open the windows, turned up the stereo, and got busy. I streaked my dog's fur with turquoise paint, just around his neck and face, with only a bit on the end of his tail. He looked great, nothing at all like the dogs inside. I laughed while dancing and painting and singing songs of such meaningfulness that the world and the black dogs became still to listen. I became drunk with wisdom and clarity that made me understand everything in the whole godforsaken world.

When I showed up for an appointment at the mental health center in an acute phase, the staff was decidedly unimpressed with my transcendence. They took me off the Elavil, cold turkey, and put me on lithium. I spent a nice week going through withdrawal from the Elavil and fighting nausea and the shakes until they got my lithium level stabilized. Pushed from behind, I started on my way back to being nothing special at all.

Somewhere in the middle of all that, I told Mike to get the hell away from me and leave me alone. It wasn't his comfort I wanted, and so his solicitousness made me feel like an invalid. I was damned if I was going to be anybody's rescue project. Like a wounded animal, I snarled and attacked any attempt at aid. I would tolerate only one person's hand.

I don't remember, honestly, what brought Joe to me. I just know I was huddled on my back deck, chain-smoking and trying to keep down the coffee I was mainlining, when he appeared and sat down. He waited patiently until I could break my thirty-yard stare and ask him what was up.

Joe talked to me quietly and calmly. He told me he was at the end of his rope with me. It was time I quit doing drugs and gave the legal ones a chance to do their job. He told me I had gone far past the point where he could look out for me anymore. Joe said I was to quit playing games with the therapists and get to work getting well.

"Son, sooner or later, it all comes down to you," he said gently. "You can live your whole life like this." Joe shuddered visibly. "God knows, I know." He stood and said he had to get going. I stood as well and stepped into him for a hug. "I'm sorry," I said. He hugged me obligingly and then held me back by my shoulders. "Don't worry about being sorry. Just get on with it. I don't have any patience left," he said. With that he was gone.

I can't say I was much of anything but a mess for a few years after that. But I did quit living off bong hits, cigarettes, and black coffee. I kept my therapy appointments and surrendered to the new script for Asendin to balance the lithium. With my brain chemistry properly tweaked, I stared down the black dogs and went to work on getting well. I went to the gym. I drank only orange juice and water. I quit smoking pot, well, regularly. I took Joe's kick in the ass as gospel. As much as I resented the hand extended, I took it.

I didn't know Joe's grandmother had been severely clinically depressed for most of her life. I only knew her as the old woman in Joe's mother's back parlor. I thought she was just mean and senile. I had no way of knowing she'd given Joe a lifetime's worth of experience in dealing with my mental disarray. She was me, minus the glaring wit and desperate entertaining charm of my manic affect.

I also didn't know Joe's life was coming slowly unglued. Jack had stayed on through the winter, living off Joe's good graces, which were ensured by the carefully rationed benefit of his dick. He was a slob. He left the hot iron on the antique dining table. He fell behind in his bills and then stopped even the pretense of paying them. Finally, he got a better offer and booked.

Joe is a practical romantic. By that time, he was a battle-hardened veteran in these physical invasions and emotional occupations. While I practiced the emotional equivalent of Stalin's scorched earth policy, Joe declared himself an open city and dealt with the consequences of watching the flags change.

For all of that, Jack's tenure in his life triggered an emotional weariness. It was just one more burden to bear in a long accumulation of disappointment on top of cheerful resignation. And the load of disappointment wasn't limited to affairs of the heart.

Joe was handed a healthy business that had been plundered by his mother's remorseless consolidation of her financial security. What he really got was a well-respected name, an excellent credit rating, and a list of contacts. For a businessman, that represented the possibilities of riches. But Joe had no practical training as a businessman. He had no more experience in running a business than a six-year-old steering a car while seated on his father's knee. His hands might have been on the wheel, but he never really drove the car.

Still the middle child, Joe had older brothers who seemingly excelled with the gifts presented to them as a legacy. He didn't know his eldest brother was experiencing the power of the car he was trying to drive as desperately as Joe was. His next older brother was, and is, a genius. Gifted with economic discernment and a calculating wisdom, he wisely stood back to let the dust settle where it may.

Joe's younger siblings found their lives disintegrating in various ways. His mother had no more finesse in handling the great affairs of this beleaguered family state than a female Beria. Without the steadying influence of Joe senior's broad hand, Joe's world dissolved into a sort of familial cold war. A proper Virginian détente was reached, but it was everyone for themselves. In that climate lay collapse for some. Joe was one.

With a client base consisting of conniving white trash who were suddenly swimming in money or the canny, threadbare aristocracy, Joe couldn't collect his receivables. Even that client base was a limited commodity in a county on the extreme edge of the earth. Supporting himself, a design assistant, a delivery man, and casual laborer like me, he couldn't meet his payables. Dispirited at the effort he didn't want to make in the first place, it all went to hell.

Unfortunately, the business didn't go quickly. It survived long enough for Joe to attempt the creation of a middle-class life— mortgage, a car payment, dreams that refused to die for a gay man in that barren place, at that bleak time.

When the business finally died, Joe joined the ranks of one of the most optimistic and ill-defined occupations of all. His business card now read "Consultant." Joe did marketing consulting on a piecemeal basis and interior design consulting for the few clients he had who actually paid their bills. With all the enthusiasm of his new profession, he agreed to take on an assignment that led to his old love. He became producer-director of a regional theater's production of the musical *Sweeney Todd: The Demon Barber of Fleet Street.*

New beginnings are heady things. New towns offer all the opportunities of being a novelty. Joe went to Wilmington to mount the production and every good-looking twink that came his way. He gathered much critical praise, publicly and privately. Triumphant, he came home to Kill Devil Hills with well wishes, a renewed spirit, and hepatitis.

As a part of my own tenuous recovery, I had made an effort at a new life and new city myself. More in an effort to hide from Rick and the weight of memories lingering on the beach, I'd moved to Raleigh. Professionally and personally, I was meeting with some success. I was making new friends, going out, and working some great freelance jobs. Then, Rick and I found each other again.

I lost my footing in my new world. My freelance jobs dried up. Still medicated and walking a very high tightrope, I decided to go home to the beach where I felt safe. I got a job working for one of the biggest bastards I've even known, but it was my ticket home. I moved back in with Joe.

I never intended to stay with Joe permanently. I was just going to crash there for a month until I could find a place of my own. Joe welcomed me back home, and we settled into what seemed a normal routine. I was completely unaware of the bitterness surrounding the closing of the shop. I never asked. Joe didn't offer any but the briefest explanation. The subject was old news. Then Joe came home one day with some fresh news.

He told me he'd not been well, which I knew, but hadn't really paid any attention to. Joe said he'd had some tests and it turned out he had hepatitis. I asked him if it was the contagious kind. Joe nodded. "I told the doctor I had a roommate who was not a sexual partner. She told me what to do to keep you from contracting it," Joe said calmly.

"So, what do I need to do?" I asked blithely. Joe sighed. "Don't drink behind me. Don't eat off my plate. Don't use my towels or washcloths. Pretty much, that's it." I shrugged. It sounded to me like it was no big deal. "Can you still cook?" I asked, suddenly concerned. Joe gave a small bitter chuckle. "Yeah, it's not that kind of hepatitis. As long as I'm careful, it shouldn't be a problem."

"What do you mean by careful?" I was reading an Anne Rice novel and only half listening. Joe said, "I can't cum in the cole slaw anymore." I cleft my attention from the book to offer up a small laugh. "I'm going to bed; I can't stand up anymore," Joe said, with genuine exhaustion leaking around the corners of his forced cheerfulness. "Are you okay?" I asked him as he stood. "No, but I'll be all right," he said. "Okay, holler if you need anything," I offered up stingily, my attention already consumed by the exploits of the vampire Lestat.

Joe's illness was stealthy. It grew so subtly that it seemed to be something else, or something else again. It didn't exactly behave like hepatitis, and that gave everyone some pause. Everyone but me. I went on with the practiced focus of someone who is functioning through a drug. With lithium providing a wall to my left and Asendin providing a wall to my right, I had a clear path to walk. I never noticed the drugs obstructing any meaningful view of the people around me.

I moved out of Joe's house as I'd planned, having found a house to rent in my old neighborhood. By the time I left, things had gotten a little tense. With all the arrogance of a recovering invalid, I thought Joe was malingering. He wasn't what I needed him to be. He wasn't the same strong guide he'd always been. I wanted him to get well and get on with supporting me emotionally. When he didn't, I dismissed him and went my merry way.

Joe was racked by inexplicable fevers. He was spared none of hepatitis's more conventional torments. But for Trent Lewis, he went through it mostly alone. Disease is more an absolute reduction of being than an overabundance of illness. Inexorably, it reduces you to your elemental self. At that point, when there is nothing left but the effort to continue to be, you find a certain pureness of purpose. When the disease has become its most complete, you are left with one decision, one request.

Many years later, Joe recalls being alone, at home. The night sweats and fevers had burned away everything; there wasn't much to recover, physically, professionally, or personally. The disease had even claimed the ability of the doctors to identify it. Joe said, "That's it. I'm ready to go." Faced with utter acceptance of the loss of the one thing he had left, he made a decision. Joe says, unequivocally, that was when he started to get well.

How is it that we have to be broken utterly to begin again? Robbed of our self-assurance, stripped of our pride, broken down to the single sure component of who we are, we do begin again. Even blind, destiny is tenacious.

While Joe was ill, my own self-absorbed little world fell apart as well. My control of it had been tenuous at best. I got in a big pissing match with the boss's art director lapdog. I was fired two days before Christmas. I went home for the holiday, and while swimming laps, my lung collapsed. I thought it was a cramp. I ended up in the hospital.

Jobless, physically weak, and disassociative once again, I did something I'd never done before. I gave up. My dad rented a U-Haul truck and called my brother. I was bundled up and driven to the beach to collect my stuff. Mama and Daddy found a new home for Tank. At twenty-eight, I ended up where I'd left at eighteen, without even my dog to remind me of where I'd been.

Joe got better slowly. When he was just fit enough to get out of the house, his brother put him to work as a laborer on one of his construction crews. Minimum wage isn't enough to support a mortgage or a life like he had. With a great deal of compassion, his brother offered him a choice. He could bail Joe out, but to what end? Nothing would have changed. The alternative was to let it all go, an adult lifetime's worth of effort, of pride.

Ending some things isn't too bad in the cold comfort of your own decision to beggar yourself. Joe took the only part remaining of what his father left him and walked away. Joe's truest inheritance was his daddy's strength. His mother, having taken his childhood desire to become a missionary, was in Uganda. Joe moved back into her house in Suffolk.

There is a great deal of freedom in making a decision from a place of utter fiscal, physical, and emotional poverty. Living in the scratchy celluloid newsreel of your life, you know this is the critical point. Empty-handed, busted back to nothing, you fit your grown self into the shrunken confines of your childhood and try your damnedest to figure out what in the hell you're going to do next.

Chapter 11

Self-Storage

By the mid-1980s, an interesting new type of architecture began to appear on the great Tidewater plain. Land-poor farmers who had survived the agricultural bust found themselves needing alternate forms of income. Some became poultry farmers. Some became hog farmers. Those unfortunates left with land too close to the cities and towns of the region to abide the odor of either operation found an interesting new occupation. They built self-storage warehouses and became the landlords of the detritus of their neighbors' lives.

There was a great need for these stalags of stuff. Rent a closet-sized space for the baby's things and boxes of old report cards, snapshots, and silly vacation hats. Rent a tiny room for a careful collection of nails, ammonium nitrate, and bigotry. Rent a garage-sized bay for Junior and Junior's drums where Junior and his friends can play Led Zeppelin. For only $29.95 a month, you can get a space big enough to hold your possessions while your life moves blindly forward.

After circumstances have stripped you of your dreams, with grim determination, you stack boxes in dark spaces to wait for an uncertain reunion. "I'll be back," you whisper fiercely to yourself, as much as to your pots and pans and sheets and towels and thousands of memories. You close the door, snap the Yale lock, and walk away unencumbered into something both known and altogether new.

Joe moved into his mother's house and began to sort himself out. Then, something happened that set him on a course he wouldn't deviate from for the next thirteen years. In the great calculating system of the fear industry, Joe's numbers spit him into a whole new category—male, over thirty, unmarried, claims for treatment of sexually transmitted hepatitis, lab work for undetermined diagnosis—all just so many damning bits of computer code. Joe found himself with his medical insurance canceled and no other company willing to provide.

Have no delusions of security. Insurance is a business, not a best friend. The good hands can drop you before you soil them; the rock can remove itself from under your fevered feet. At that time, when HIV threatened profits, there was no justice, only us.

Lest anyone forget, or claim not to have heard, it once was not taught that it is inhuman to simply watch gay people die. Now, so many years later, politeness has been bought by death. Our government has been forced to smell the shit and hear the screams. Straight people lost their smug immunity to the bitter salt of gay tears. But in another time, understanding was thin on the ground. Freed from the constraints of self, that same time had been created for Joe to move into the world. Activism is born of injustice. Anger picked Joe up, pointed out a need, and said go.

It is hard to say whether redemption comes first from the outside or the inside. Joe looked at home and saw that Tidewater Virginia had more than a few needs in the fight against the plague. The welter of ego-driven AIDS support groups battled diverse agendas. A population of sheep were still unaware they would be the next into the abattoir without some shepherding. Another population of the uncaring had to be given bread and circuses to keep their attention, and a moribund bureaucracy needed to be slapped into awareness.

As much as I would like to cast Joe as a white knight galloping into the battle to save the day, he will not let me. What he says occurred over the course of the following years was a series of opportunities that enabled him to use some skills he had developed during his life. His work with other nonprofit organizations had provided him with experience in the dynamics of board/staff relationships. According to Joe, with that type of management and political skills, he filled a need for an organization that, in turn, provided him with a chance to apply a fundamental understanding of how nonprofit organizations function. Couple those factors with a sincere willingness to work his ass off and a great deal of change was effected.

Now, working on his doctorate in business administration, Joe perceives that whole time with a broader perspective: "It was hard because we were in the middle of an epidemic and a lot of well-meaning people with egos overfed by their own entrepreneurial successes always knew a better way to do things. That was, of course, their way," Joe recalls, then chuckles. "I learned a lot of political skills in that job."

Joe is also more reserved about his accomplishments than I would be, representing one of the thousands who stood outside the fray and simply mailed off checks. In assessing his effectiveness in the fight, Joe feels he addressed more things than he accomplished: "Accomplishment can be measured in different ways, and perhaps I did accomplish some things, but now the interesting thing that asserts itself is the lack of yardsticks we had to measure any accomplishment at all," he muses.

Following his years working for the nonprofit organization, Joe was recruited to work in the administrative area of the provision of HIV-related services for the Eastern Virginia Medical School, in Norfolk: "In my work at the medical school, I was able to develop some measuring tools for program evaluation," he explains.

Everyone has an image of the soldiers in the guerrilla action against the plague as being the patient's immediate care provider. Unfortunately, while that is an accurate perception, it's not the only one.

In the provision of health services to HIV-infected individuals, a great bureaucracy and industry sprang up following the scent of money that covered the stench of suffering and death. Every layer of government that threw a stingy guilt offering of money at the effort required voluminous evidence that their money was being well spent. The drug companies and insurance companies and even the physicians clamored for justification of their efforts and funding.

The popular image is of the selfless volunteer appearing with a hot meal, but before that, there had to be a person to beg someone else for money to buy the food and then justify the need for the meal. "I met fierce resistance from the individual providers because there was a common battle cry that they were the ones doing things—why quibble about whether or not their effort was satisfactory—why worry about program evaluation when people were dying," Joe explains.

The simple fact was, the powers that be who funded all those collective efforts demanded quantifiable results. They still do. The gods of bureaucracy do not see individuals; they see numbers. The people who can translate the suffering of people to propitiate those callous gods are no less heroes than the ones who whisper comfort to the dying.

A little boy sits on a church bench. Peculiar to one place and time, he is made up of bits and pieces of steadiness and strength, patience and talent. God whispers in his ear, tugs at his imagination, and then walks away. Years pass in dreaming and dancing and living and paying the rent, with those words dismissed and forgotten. But nothing is for no reason.

So many of the particulars of this time in Joe's life are missing for me. We have now spent more time together over phone, fax, and e-mail than we probably did when living in the same town. I was privy to those times only by way of the phone. Joe would speak of a function, a frustration, a tiny victory, and a larger loss. In my visits, he was more likely to dismiss the details of his activism in favor of the comfort of discussions of the past.

What I was aware of, and what I have seen, are the results of those years. Through his sweat and aching head, medicines have been provided, education has been extended and accepted, lives have been changed, lost ones have been sent on their way in peace.

The public man who has been my friend has let so many more than me crawl up his backbone to a place they had to reach. I see the private man smile. More than work redeems. There is also love. Often you can give so much that you get something in return to keep. By stepping outside of himself into the world of others, Joe found himself richer, waiting for himself back where he began.

I, on the other hand, found myself by coming back into myself. If, by now, my nature hasn't revealed itself as being one of self-absorption, it certainly should have come off as self-motivating. Finding myself back home as an adult child, my self-reliance was brought low. Facing the reality of the necessity of being home, I concluded that it was my foray into the world of other people that got me fucked up in the first place.

With Mom and Dad providing me a stable surface on which to regain my footing, I saw myself as sort of a born-again teenager. My return to a pseudoadolescence was the result of getting it so wrong the first time. I figured I now had a chance to fix what I'd broken the last time around. At least time had shown me what I didn't want, even if it had taken away what I did.

My dad laid down the law that he wouldn't tolerate any drugs in the house, except for the ones the doctor prescribed. I stayed with the whole antidepressant regimen, but I refused to go back to a shrink. Fortunately, the doctor I'd been seeing since I was an infant had an intimate knowledge of manic-depressive illness. He stepped up to the plate and kept me on lithium and Asendin.

On that much medication, I had to watch out for side effects. The worst was being the human equivalent of a neutered tomcat. All I wanted to do was lie in the sun and sleep. I had come home looking like an Andean air crash survivor, so my mom decided I needed to eat. To avoid turning into a triple-sized version of myself, I joined the Y.

Swimming has always been a big thing to me. I have always had a level of ease in the water that I never have on land. This eccentric lady I knew years later did my whole natal astrological chart. It seems where and when I was born, the moon was in Cancer. I am a Cancer with a Cancer rising and a Pisces ascendant. All water signs. In an easy way, that explains the stormy years on antidepressants and an affinity for anything aquatic. In any event, I swam every day and did aerobics with a bunch of straight women every other day. Which helped with another problem.

As well as being a born-again teenager, I was a born-again virgin. Between the stupefying effects of the meds, my constant exercise, and my complete segregation from any sort of erotic life, I didn't care if I got laid or not. As far as I was concerned, I needed the break. I had spent my share of innocence. Emotionally bankrupt, I needed some time to build up my reserves.

At first, I spent any time I wasn't working or swimming just hanging out. Mom and Dad hadn't seen too much of me over the years. I blew in and out of town every once in awhile, but, basically, my attitude was, "I'm okay, you're okay, okay? Now, get the hell out of my way." For the first couple months I was back, they seemed to delight in just having me around. Right then, I was so numb, I basically just sat and stared out the back door. However, if nature abhors a vacuum, my mother abhors an unresponsive child. She talked nonstop until I started talking back. Gently, Dad got me into playing cards with him and Mom, if only to pull my focus to a different view.

They knew I was crazy as hell, but they had no idea how high-functioning I was. Every day, I got up, went to work, swam, came home. Every day. Like a little machine, just wind me up and set me loose. Routine is a great comfort, when you've spun out, offering freedom from having to think about anything but drawing a straight line, counting laps, or walking into the void of sleep. Slowly, I came back to life.

One Sunday in late January, my dad showed me an ad in the local paper that announced a call for entries for a community art show. He encouraged me to enter it. "Hell, son, you got enough crap in your storage unit, you don't even have to do anything new," he said. I told him I'd think about it.

The next Saturday afternoon, I drove out to where I'd stored my old self. I sat in my truck for a half hour listening to the kids a few bays over torture "Kashmir" out of two Peavey amps. I didn't really want to go through all that stuff. It just reminded me that my life was on hold.

Finally, I worked up the nerve to open the unit and root around. I found the box with all my acrylics in it. I found my brushes. I found a largish piece of Masonite I'd already gessoed that was in good shape. I threw all of that stuff in the back of the truck and went back for my easel.

At home, Mom was less than enthusiastic. She'd been to my houses before. I tended to turn anywhere I lived into a studio, with paint all over everything and often myself. I promised her I'd be neat. I had an idea for the first time in a long time. I sketched out a pool and a diver that afternoon. Hating it, I changed the figure so that it was ambiguous as to whether he was falling into or bursting out of the water. I fell into the painting myself. It felt good. Steadily my life adjusted to a new routine; work, swim, paint, sleep. My field of focus was widening incrementally.

The art show was really a cattle call. Everybody in the county who could hold a brush seemed to have entered a painting of a sad clown, a psychotic bowl of fruit, or portraits of Jesus or Waylon Jennings—I couldn't tell which. The only thing missing was Elvis. My painting was so weirdly out of place with all the other stuff, I was really dismayed. It vividly pointed out how much of an outsider I was and always had been. Fortunately, I went alone. I left rather quickly for the pristine near emptiness of the pool at the Y.

Later the following week, the director of the community art center called me. She was impressed with my painting and wanted to extend an invitation to participate in a group show at the gallery in June. She said it had to be recent work, then asked how many pieces and what size and medium I could show. I told her six, all 32″ × 46″, all acrylics on Masonite, all framed. She was delighted and told me she'd be in touch with the details.

I said, "Cool," and hung up the phone. Somewhere in that conversation I'd discovered two things I'd lost: a set of balls the size of avocados (I had no new work) and a fierce desire to kick some artistic ass. The rush felt strange. I knew I was too drugged for this to be a manic episode. The surprise was that this small, but necessary, part of me had come kicking and screaming back to life.

Joe and Trent Lewis drove three hours down Highway 13 for the opening of the show. It was worth it. I dominated. My pieces were so big that they overpowered the petite landscapes, tortured wood sculptures, and timid assemblages of the other three artists. My paintings of men against huge skies were in your face and disturbing. These were my first attempts at photorealism and I hated the results, but it felt good to be slinging paint around again.

Joe and I didn't get to talk much in the opening throng. But he looked great. He looked strong. He had regained that sense of presence that preceded him into a room. With a glass of white wine in one hand, I watched him become a magnet in the crowded gallery. People were drawn to his confident laugh and hypnotized by his charm. My Joe was back.

I slipped outside for a cigarette. I have always weirded out quickly in crowds, my meds making me feel as if I am about three sentences behind in any conversation. Things were still too tenuous and tender in my head to allow for the sharp parry and thrust of so many strangers' personalities. Much discipline is needed to sparkle. Despite the obvious success of the evening, I wanted to be alone, outside of it.

"Hey, baby. You're a hit. You need to come back inside," said Joe, handing me a fresh glass of white wine. "Do you like the paintings?" I asked anxiously. "Can you tell I've been working? Do you think they're any good?" I begged, without waiting for an answer.

Joe chuckled. "I think you scare the hell out of the locals." I felt an easy smile grow. I lit a cigarette and looked back inside at all the people who had been frightening me only moments before. "I think it's some of your best work," Joe said decisively.

"You ain't just saying that to keep me out of the razor blades are you?" I rejoined. Joe shook his head. "I already have the one I want picked out." I felt too fragile for compliments. "They all suck," I said. "They do not," Joe rejoined quickly. "Don't be so goddamn down on yourself, boy." I gave him a half smile. "It's hard," I said simply. "I know, baby. I know," Joe replied gently.

I took a deep hit off my cigarette and looked away. When I could trust my voice, I said, "You look great." Joe laughed. "I don't know how you can say that. I have been eating like a hog. I could hardly get these drawers up over these childbearing hips."

I joined his laughter then. "God, I miss you," I said. Joe drew me into a hug. "I miss you too," he said. I felt homesick then, but I also felt stronger. Joe gave off strength like some people give off anger and attitude. When he let me go, I said, disbelieving, "Everything's going to be okay, isn't it?" Joe laughed gently. "It already is. C'mon. You need to get back inside and meet your public." I smiled and took a last hit off my cigarette. "Philistines," I said and flicked away what was left of the cigarette. "Hmmm, that's a big ol' word," Joe said as he steered me back into the gallery and a little further toward getting well.

Joe and Trent went back to their own lives, and I stumbled along with mine, a smudge of cadmium yellow under my hollowed-out eyes and phthalo blue under my fingernails. Joe, it seemed, had more to go home to than just the efforts to keep the plague at bay. The aircraft carrier that Brad was stationed on was on its way back to Norfolk, bringing not only Brad but a future that Joe couldn't have foreseen for himself.

Comfortably but inconveniently ensconced in Joe's mother's home in Suffolk, Joe and Brad expanded a courtship in person that had begun as just another trick on a lonesome winter night and grew in long letters across an ocean's expanse. Joe's mother's approaching return from her missionary duties in Uganda forced their decision to live together. They began to look for a place to share, closer to both their jobs in Norfolk, but still away from too-prying eyes. Portsmouth fit the bill on many different levels.

Old Town Portsmouth is patinaed without being precious. The gracious old town homes with their cobblestone streets cling around the harborside opposite Norfolk like lace on a petticoat. Portsmouth is not the precious flower of the South that her cousins Charleston and Savannah are. She's a sailor's wife, and she has the gentility of humor and long patience, not rigid practice.

In a one-hundred-fifty-year-old town house in Old Town, Joe and Brad found a harbor and started a home. The gracious old rooms and verandahs expanded to include me and Trent Lewis and closed to allow Joe and Brad the intimacy needed to create a life for each other. It was a warm and wonderful place, with candlelight and gladiolas again on the sideboard in Joe's dining room. Cocktails and dinner conversation warmed the old rooms as Brad and Joe created the home both had been seeking, but couldn't make alone.

Bravely, Brad reclaimed Joe's life from self-storage like bidding at a warehouse auction. He has always had the extraordinary ability to find great treasure behind long-worn doors, a gift that made itself useful in many ways. No one else in Joe's life had ever bothered to look into the rooms hidden away and choked with dust and cobwebs. Brad opened the windows and welcomed in the breezes.

The Portsmouth house grew too small for the burgeoning richness of their lives together. The dogs needed a yard. The couple needed to stretch themselves into a challenge that was larger than the narrow focus on each other. Vested for the first time in his life, with a home of his own making, Joe took Brad to the home he had lived in on suffrage for his early life. Joe and Brad bought an eighty-five-year-old spinster of a house in Suffolk and turned her into the talk of the town.

Picking out wallpaper and refinishing floors has a certain significance that is somehow too subtle for many straight people to cherish. Deprived of building a life around progeny, gay couples build lives of actual mortar, wood, and stone. The longevity of the built world is both a symbol and a goal. Then, too, there is truth in the old adage that advises people to do two things before marrying: hang a picture and buy a sofa together.

Paint and patience, plumbing and passion, tile and tears, lawn furniture and laughter are just the beginning of a list for living and loving someone long and well. That is something I learned from Joe and Brad. Every chance I could, I found my way to Suffolk. Each new effort they tackled and resolved taught me lessons I had long given up on learning.

My life didn't advance from the arithmetic Rick and I had practiced. I watched Joe and Brad move from those basic equations of the heart to a kind of calculus of complementary sums. My sexual statistics grew as I regained my urge to live past pool, paint, and canvas. But I had never been good at the math that Joe and Brad were mastering. My equations totaled alone, not a home.

As Joe and Brad were solving the complex problems of building their life together, I moved from Mom and Dad's to other towns and other cities. I chased my solitary dreams and shared nobody's bed for long. About the time Joe and Brad were planting a rose garden and bulbs, I was thinking of moving along again.

I had played out Raleigh. At first, I was strong and unafraid enough to wean myself off the Asendin. I'd been in that fog long enough. Though I was still not bad crazy, thanks to the lithium, I had not become lost, but I had idled along the way. I didn't really know what I was doing anymore. My great creative efforts were thwarted by their utter lack of meaning to the wider world of that community. I'd run out of steam.

I said fuck it and took a job as a pool boy/lifeguard for a summer. While recaulking tile or cleaning skimmers, I tried to figure out what to do next. I played pool games with elementary school kids and thought about my life. With little kids flashing in the air as I tossed them, gleaming like slick, brown dolphins in the summer sun, I drew some conclusions.

I worked odd hours at the pool. Arriving at eight in the mornings, I swam laps for a half hour. From eight-thirty to ten, I did maintenance and then taught swimming lessons until two in the afternoon. From two to five-thirty, I went home and messed around drawing, reading, and napping. From six to nine, I was back at the pool for free swim and lockdown.

I wasn't really seeing anyone. Occasionally, I had sex with a US Air ramper from Raleigh-Durham International, and about as often with a six-five real estate stud who took me out for sushi and had a thing for rape fantasies. All in all, it was a pleasant, superficial life. I dreaded Labor Day and the emptiness beyond it. I was turning thirty-three, I was just drifting, and I knew it.

I didn't see Joe and Brad for that whole summer. I told myself it was because of my odd hours at the pool; the truth was, in comparison to their life together, I was treading water. Joe had moved into the medical administration area of the delivery of HIV treatment. Brad had just gotten a job as a librarian, which he found rewarding. Working together, their house was becoming a late-Italianate-with-vernacular-adaptations confection.

I had a really cool halyard for my whistle and bruises under my tan from the playacting with the sushi date rapist. My life was bullshit. Three things dovetailed to motivate me to get off my ass. Singly, they might not have worked in the same way, but together they gave me just the sharp push I needed.

He was sixteen and all elbows, knees, and bony shoulders. At six-one he still hadn't grown into his feet or hands. He had a dense, close-cropped cap of black hair, creamy skin, and a huge crush on me. He showed up early in the mornings, easily vaulting the gate I left locked. Without a word, he would jump in the pool to wet himself down and then sit on the coping at the end of the pool, dangling his legs in the water and watching me swim laps.

I would ignore him until winded, and, watchful of the clock on the front of the pool house, I'd pull myself out of the water next to his lanky form. He would start talking then and not stop for the hour it took to vacuum the pool, clean the skimmers, and get my first chlorine readings. He would lope off when the kids came for their swimming lessons.

I wouldn't see him again until closing time when I blew my whistle to clear out the working folks who were lazily sipping illicit screwdrivers and G and T's from sweaty go cups. He'd ease down the walk past the sleepy kids and their drowsy daddies padding away home over the warm concrete. He'd strip off his shirt to swim while I emptied the garbage cans, tidied up the bathrooms, and took the final chlorine readings.

I'd turn off all the lights except those in the pool. He'd buy us each a Coke from the machine by the chemical room, and we'd sit swinging our legs in the warm heavy water, sharing a joint, while he talked and talked and talked. His imagination was bigger than mine, or he had as tenuous a grasp on reality as I did. He told me he was a Mafia princeling whose father had been whacked. The big guy had sent him and his mom down to hide out in Raleigh.

His accent was pure Raleigh, with occasional, studied Long Island inflections. From one of my elderly, leathered pool lizards, I learned his mother and father were separated and noisily not reconciling. I knew he was in the gifted program at his high school but made terrible grades. I also knew I was happy just letting him talk and watching the dark hair on his legs sway in the blue-green chlorinated water.

I was sixteen once. I knew sometimes you talked to buy time because you waited all day for these moments. I remembered you talked to distract yourself from the urge to kiss the boy at your side and that you were hard just because the breeze was so warm. I recalled how an accidental brush of fingers or thighs could give invention wings so the night wouldn't be called a day, ending the electric awareness of the flesh next to you.

It was so utterly sweet. I found myself turning down sushi rape dates and rendezvous with the ramper just to sit next to this yearling boy and let his stories mingle and fade into the chirring night songs of summer insects. I let it go on until, one night, he took my hand and asked me if I'd ever thought about skinny-dipping in the pool. That was where the rubber hit the road. I told him I hadn't thought about it, but I would . . . think about it. I finished my Coke in one long swallow and smiled gently into his eager, frightened eyes. "Right now, I've got to dump some chemicals in the pool and get going, okay?" I said softly. He squeezed my fingers so hard I thought he would break them off. "It would be really cool . . . you know, one time wouldn't be any big thing, right?" he asked in an unpracticed, low, gruff voice.

Oh Christ, I thought to myself. It's no big thing. No. How do I tell this child it's just the beginning of a long, long road that brings you back to the same place when you are thirty-three and have seen things nobody should see? "Naw," I said. "One time probably would be okay. That way you'd at least know if you ever wanted to go for it again, right?" He smiled and let go of my hand to splash me. We got up laughing, and I closed down the pool for the night. "See you in the morning," he said. "For sure," I said.

When I got home, I pulled out a bottle of vodka and took it out on the back steps. I took little sips to ease the pain and panic and longing rising in my heart. I had enough sense not to get drunk. I just got greased good enough to stand the fact that I was never going to be that innocent again.

The next day started casually with our morning meeting. Nothing was said about the night before until my kindergartners and first-graders came skipping and running along the sidewalks to the still-locked gate. He gazed at me with a look so cool, it had to have been practiced. "So you think you're up for it?" he asked and looked dead in my eyes, waiting for my answer. "How about you?" I asked. He shrugged and said, "It's no big deal. I mean, it's just a good time, right?" He looked back at me uncertainly, ready to bolt or stay, depending on what I said.

The kids were calling from the gate, their floaties around their upper arms and their noses showing sunblock from a hundred yards away. He braved a grin and said, "So tonight then?" I nodded. "Sure thing," I said and tossed him my keys. "Unlock the gate for me, will ya? Give the keys to Stuart to bring back down to me," I said as he caught them. I gave him an affectionate shove and said, "Stuart's the one with the mohawk and the plastic Uzi." He got bashful suddenly and looked away as he said okay. The enormity of what he'd asked for and what he would receive made him almost get tangled in his own feet as he sprinted away.

I sailed through my morning wondering what in the hell I'd done. At best, it would be statutory rape or something. At worst, it would be prison and scandal and another hole I'd dug for myself to climb out of. After the swimming lessons, I sent my little kids home to their lunches and naps. I left the pool to the old lady lizards. Used to my routine, they barely looked up from their copies of *Love's Torrid Throbbing Savage Sweetness,* or whatever.

Back home, I mixed a protein shake and let myself chain-smoke in the air-conditioning. I was thinking it back through. I mean, I'd really be doing the kid a favor. I'd be good to him. I thought about my sushi buddy being with him for his first time and it made me nauseous. I poured the rest of my shake down the sink and went for a shower. The cool water did nothing to banish the scenarios.

Naked, I made my way into my room and lay down for my nap in the dim coolness of the closed blinds. I was horny as hell. I couldn't stop thinking about him. My hand found the most insistent part of my being and began the rhythm that justified anything, especially tall, rawboned sixteen-year-olds with sweet, sweet smiles and feet the size of johnboats.

Getting close, so close, I was interrupted by a violent explosion in the room on the other side of my bedroom wall. I lay shocked and terrified at the sudden thunder of breaking wood, plaster, and glass. When I could move from my frozen awkwardness, I pulled on some boxer shorts and ran to the front of the house to find a late-model Chevy Cavalier half in my housemate's office.

My place was on a corner lot in an older part of town. An elderly lady had run a stop sign and forced her car into my front yard, up into my front porch, and through the front wall. Luckily, no one was badly hurt. The house was pretty fucked up. I called 911 first, my landlord second, and was just getting ready to dial my housemate at work when the phone rang in my hand. It was my astrologer lady friend, out of the clear blue sky.

"Are you aware that the last solar eclipse of this century, visible in this hemisphere, just now occurred in your sign?" she asked breathlessly. A policeman carefully made his way through the hole in the front room and looked pointedly at my boxer shorts and then shook his head. "Okay, so . . ." I replied, while looking the cop in the eye and shrugging. "And you either just turned or will turn thirty-three, right?" she demanded. I said, "Yeah," and gave the cop a pleading look.

"Okay. It's like this. With this eclipse happening in your sign, so close to your Saturn return, it's a very big deal," she said breathlessly. I turned my back to the cop and said, "Okay, you got my attention." She paused, and I could almost see her peering up at the acoustic tiles over her cubicle in the huge office on Six Forks Road where she worked as a temp. "Have you been thinking of moving?" she demanded. "Not just across town, but a long distance away?"

Now it was my turn to pause. "Well, yeah. I mean, I haven't told anybody or decided or anything. But I have been thinking of moving to Florida," I said. The cop slipped on some broken glass and crashed into my housemate's bookcase. "What was that?" my psychic astrologer friend asked. "It was a policeman slipping on some glass. A car just crashed into my house," I said. "My God. What do you have to be, hit over the head? Run out of town on a rail? Forced away at gunpoint?" she gasped.

"What in the hell are you talking about?" I almost screamed. "This all happens in your home comfort security area," she said. "You have to move. It'll be the best thing that ever happened to you. It's, like, destiny," she whispered in awe.

That night, I cleaned up the pool area alone. I sat and had my Coke, not so much waiting for my sweet young'un to show up as to ponder the inevitable. I had been talking with some friends of mine who were moving to South Beach. They had offered me a room in their apartment if I'd move down with them. I had just closed a freelance deal that would earn me a nice piece of change in a few weeks. I could live off that money for five months in Raleigh, or I could move to Miami Beach and start a new life.

My Coke can held cigarette butts. The clock on the pool house wall said two hours had gone by. He obviously wasn't coming. I figured that was for the best. If my life was regressing to the point that I was having a summer romance with a sixteen-year-old, I needed to get my ass out of Dodge. I mixed some powdered chlorine in a bucket of water and distributed it evenly from around the rim of the pool. The milky denseness of powder and water slid into the turquoise like an avalanche of hope and longing, dissolving suddenly and fading to nothing.

I didn't see my boy anymore. He stopped coming around. One of my old ladies told me he'd gotten a job working in a record store at the mall. I decided that was a good thing. I'd begun my freelance graphic design assignment, with the decision made to leave Raleigh right after I helped shut down the pool, right after Labor Day.

I spent my last week at the pool weaving thin red and white cording into friendship bracelets for all my kids. School had started, but we were going to get together for a little swimming lesson graduation ceremony my final Saturday of work. The Thursday morning before graduation day, it rained like it wasn't ever going to stop. I concentrated on my bracelets and went over my packing list in my head. I wasn't going to put anything in self-storage. What I didn't need or want anymore, I was going to let go and walk away.

I looked up when I heard somebody kicking at the door. He was standing out in the rain with two McDonald's coffee cups and a sodden bag. I let him in. "I brought you some breakfast," he said, dripping. I took the soggy breakfast from him, then tossed him a towel from the lost-and-found box. "Help yourself," he said as he rubbed the wet out of his hair. "I really just want the coffee," I replied. He moved to the table, examining with studied curiosity my bracelet-making stuff, which was laid out in neat rows.

I sat down and dumped some creamer and a couple packs of sugar into the steaming cup. "Shouldn't you be in school?" I asked as he straddled a folding chair across the table from me. "I wanted to say good-bye," he said. I nodded and picked up the bracelet I'd been working on when he arrived. "Those are so cool," he said, watching me twist the cords into a flat, narrow band a quarter-inch wide.

"They're for the kids," I explained. He nodded and looked behind him out at the rain curtaining the glass front of the pool house. Turning back, he pushed the wet bag of food away abruptly, then toyed with his coffee. "I wanted to, but I couldn't," he said without preamble. "Me too," I replied, "but it needed to be right for you." I smoothed out the new work between my thumb and fingers. I looked up at him and said, "It's not a problem, okay?" He hunched over his coffee and looked back at me through wet, impossibly thick, black lashes.

I looped the last threads of the bracelet together and pulled tight the complicated knot. "It wasn't you. I still think you're so hot, it's just . . . " he said as he rocked on the chair's back legs and looked away too quickly. He started to tumble backward. I reached across the table, grabbing him by a flailing wrist, and pulled him back. Securely on all four legs once again, I marveled at the slender wrist that broadened into such huge hands as I let go. He reached across the table, took my hand, and squeezed it.

I smiled at him and slid my fingers from his sweaty grip. I looked on the table amid the bracelets for the longest one I could find. I'd made one for myself, thinking the kids and I could stay tied together, somehow. The bracelets would be a reminder of the summer as the threads got dirty and finally worn through so that you don't feel it as it finally falls away and is lost for good. I took his hand back and tied the red-and-white striped bracelet around his wrist.

"It was the best summer I've had in a long, long time, baby," I said. "You made a lot of things right you didn't even know were wrong," I told him. He looked at me with his heart's first questioning "what if." Contented to be that first in his life, I squeezed his wrist above the brightly woven threads. "Thanks," I said and let him go.

I didn't have too many good-byes to say in Raleigh after the ones to my summer kids. Some very important ones remained to be said elsewhere before I headed south down I-95. With my car packed, I headed north first, to Suffolk and Joe and Brad. I found they had grown into each other in an amazing way. They shared an intimacy between them that I had never seen before. As with two people who have lived together a long time, they completed each other's unspoken thoughts. Like Baucis and Philemon, the gods had granted them the favor of spreading from a single trunk into two very different trees.

It wasn't envy I felt—not for the comfort they shared with each other, nor for their lives or the beautiful house they made and shared. It was just a longing I hadn't fulfilled, certainly not with my work or my loves that came and went with intensity and finished so finally. In many ways, so much of the best of me was still in self-storage, waiting in the dimness to be reclaimed. I figured, whether I was in Raleigh or Miami, waiting was the same; only the quality of dimness could change.

Chapter 12

Troth

He was just a junior manager at Hardee's, a regional burger chain. His lover was somewhat more successful, being the co-owner of a popular home accessories store. I knew them slightly through a mutual friend who was an attorney. The couple had been lovers for some time when the more successful one became ill. His lover stuck with him to the bitter end. For his trust and fidelity, and certainly for his love, the dying one made a will leaving all of their possessions to his surviving mate.

The end wasn't anything to inspire faithfulness. Brain lesions caused dementia, blindness, and a great deal of unfocused rage. The family appeared, of course, for the end and epilogue. While everyone was at the funeral, the deceased's mother had the locks changed, the utilities turned off, and an off-duty policeman paid to guard the home her son and his lover shared.

When the lover came home from the funeral, he had to call our friend the attorney to get a court order allowing him access to his own home. He was allowed in once, under armed escort, to get his clothes, nothing else. His lover's mother had the will vacated on the grounds of dementia and undue influence. She got everything. If there is a god, the swine in hell will eat her soul.

In 1992 on a sunny Saturday afternoon in late October, I anxiously dialed Joe and Brad's house from my apartment in South Beach, hoping somebody would answer the phone. I couldn't remember if it started at three or four. Knowing how those two revered tradition and etiquette, I was suprised it wasn't going to be at eight in the evening. Even I knew that was when the most formal of weddings took place.

Technically, this wasn't a wedding. Joe and Brad's church performed weddings with certainty. It performed another type of ceremony with solemn indulgence. For Joe and Brad, that indulgence confirmed their commitment to that church and each other. However, a union ceremony was the spiritual equivalent of the wedding rites, if not legally recognized under any state's law. Joe and that skittish young trick who answered the door all those years ago were going to tie the knot in front of God and all those assembled.

Except for me. Near broke, but a survivor of a nasty hit-and-run accident, two surgeries, and Hurricane Andrew, I couldn't get to Suffolk, and I wanted badly to be there. I didn't feel one way or the other about the ceremony itself, but I knew and respected how much it meant to Joe and Brad. The best I could do was make the same teasing visit to the dressing rooms via phone that I would have made in person.

Trent Lewis picked up on the second ring. He was his usual calm, wry self as he filled me in on all the pre-event histrionics. I could close my eyes and see it all going on. I got to speak briefly to Brad, who was coming unglued with a sort of German efficiency. When Joe picked up the receiver, I said, "Hey. You knew you weren't gonna get married without me giving my blessing."

Joe's warm chuckle betrayed little more than bemusement with the whole affair. Having made his mind up to do it, he stood diffidently above his siblings and their mother's various emotional tactics to thwart the ceremony from the beginning. Of course, when push came to shove, they'd rather have died than not attended. The house's decorations and reception treats alone would be worth a lifetime of finely crafted darts to be flung at just the most effective moment.

"How's your mom handling it?" I asked hesitantly. "She's here and she looks fabulous," Joe confided. "She is doing a lot better than she did at my sister's wedding." I felt happy just thinking about it. Joe's mother is actually a lovely woman with more personal presence than our past three reigning First Ladies combined. I could see her taking charge with the firm belief that if the travesty was going to be done, by God, it would be done right.

I heard someone call Joe in the background. I said, "I love you, Daddy Joe and I love Brad too. I know you got to go. God bless." I heard Joe cover the phone with his hand and offer a clipped response to whoever was summoning him. Then he spoke to me.

"Thank you so much. Actually, I wanted you to be the ring bearer, my child from an earlier marriage. Appropriate, don't you think?" I laughed. Seriously, he said, "I wish you could be here." I could almost smell the fresh flowers that were bedecking the staircase. "Look in your shirt pocket. I'm right in there, next to your heart," I said.

From all subsequent accounts, Joe and Brad's union ceremony was the avatar of taste, loveliness, and genuine celebration. Even alone, a thousand miles south of Broad Street that afternoon, I could feel the joy. Once again, Joe had made the way ahead of me, showing me at least one way to go.

I got there myself, but without the ceremony or the flowers. I have screamed at my partner, Jeff, exactly three times in (at this point) seven years. Two of those times had to do with the purchase of a house. When we first decided to live together, Jeff had taken me into his home and never acted as though it was anything but ours for the five years we had lived together. But something inside me still needed the security of having my name on the papers.

When we were making the rules that came to govern our lives together, I told Jeff, "Two things break up any couple, gay or straight. Cheating and money. If we get those two things figured out before we start, we ought to be set for good." He agreed.

As part of the money negotiations, I told Jeff, right off the bat, that his house was *his* house. He bought it long before I was in the picture, and I would never give him any grief about what he did with it. In the flush of first love, I recall telling him I'd live with him anywhere. If he wanted to sell the damn house and move us into a trailer park, I'd go with him. I never changed my mind. I made one amendment to that statement: the proviso that the next house would be ours, together.

Five years later, we found a great house we both really wanted and started the nightmare of buying a home. I swear, I'd rather chew on tin foil and comb my hair with a cheese grater than go through that process again anytime soon. For all the frustration, nail biting, and angst, it still marks a new phase of your adulthood. As a benchmark in my life and ours together, I was really looking forward to the closing.

The night before the scheduled closing, Jeff and I were still trying to pack up the house. Jeff has never thrown away as much as a gum wrapper in his life. The dogs sensed something was up and were in a fit of neurotic barking, hurling their ninety-pound selves against the windows to attack passersby. In the midst of this, a good friend of ours who was going to do the closing for us called and suggested we skip the formal meeting. She offered to drive around to all the parties concerned, individually, to collect all the signatures on all the papers.

Jeff held up the phone and presented the idea to me. I blew up. I said I had made enough concessions to every nasty little gobbler in the whole goddamn real estate food chain, and, by God, I would have a formal closing, in a conference room, with every single motherfucker who was supposed to be there in attendance. When provoked, Jeff can give as good as he gets. He started yelling back, asking me why I was being so difficult.

When I could get a word in edgewise, I shouted, "Because I never got a goddamn wedding. I want somebody legal to acknowledge just what the hell I'm doing with you and my life." Jeff yelled back that I was being a child. "Yeah? Well fuck this and fuck you," I shouted and then slammed out the door.

He found me sitting on the hood of a car in front of the house. I looked at him, warningly. He held up his hands in surrender and said, "I had no idea this meant so much to you." I shrugged it off. "You should have said something, Jay," he scolded softly. I just rubbed my temples and looked down the street.

"The closing's at six. In the conference room of the realtor's office. Everybody will be there," he said gently. "Thanks," I replied, mollified. "C'mon back in the house and do something with your dogs. I think Travis just peed on a box of towels," he said and reached out for my hand. I took it and slid off the hood of the car. We went back in and finished packing.

The next evening, I was the last person after Jeff to sign the last line on the last sheet on a set of forms and copies of forms that must have destroyed an entire forest. A deep thrill ran through me. I held up the paper for Jeff to see and said, "I've got papers on you now. If you want me out, you've got to buy me out. Nobody can take this away from me." The realtors and the elderly couple we bought the house from looked at me nervously. Jeff snorted. "Nobody but the bank. Congratulations, humphead. You're in debt."

With that, our realtor presented us with a gift box of Perrier Jouët Fleurs with two glasses. "Congratulations on your new home," she said sincerely. "Mazel tov," said the sellers. "Good luck, guys," said the seller's agent. "God bless us, every one," our friend and closing agent said. With that benediction, Jeff squeezed my thigh under the table and gave me a wink and a smile. For me, that was as good as I ever wanted to get.

The reality of marriage lies, after all, in fulfilling the contract, not in the contract or paper it's written on. A marriage really consists of the effort and satisfaction in the constant accommodation, cooperation, and consideration to, with, and for another human being. Don't talk to me about the party; talk to me about the cleaning up after it, paying for it, and going through the pictures of it years later with a shared sense of hard-won humor and pride.

Of course, the practical aspects of the marriage contract, such as rights, privileges, and entitlements, are extended by formal recognition of a domestic partnership. Heteronormative lawmakers who self-righteously legislate to uphold their majority's exclusive hold on the benefits of marriage are sly. They know the law is a whore; if you throw enough money at it, it will spread its legs and do what you want it to do.

Different legal entitlements are available to gay couples, and the law extends these with feigned, open-eyed innocence of their implication. Corporations formed by two adults are recognized by law with the same rights and respect afforded marriage. For gay couples, various powers of attorney provide legal assurance of the sanctity of each member's right to determination in regard to the other's health care, money, and property. With the proper wording of warranty deeds, there is no discussion of what belongs to whom. And, most certainly, when it comes to money, if a houseplant can qualify and cosign a loan agreement, any bank will write the check.

Of course, I believe that gay people should be entitled to having their marriages extended the same recognition under the law that straight people enjoy. Bill Clinton's signature on the Defense of Marriage Act entitles him to a special black eye in the long view of history. Such hastily proglumated and obviously prejudicial acts of jurisprudence will ultimately go the same way as those which once defined African Americans as property. Such an act stands as an embarrassment in complete contradiction of what America is supposed to be.

Until then, I piss on the right to marry. I piss on the whole presumption of equal protection under the law when it can be defined and redefined on a whim. Keep it. I'll get my justice through the back door and laugh at any legal embarrassment that ensues. As long as I have the courage to define who I love, I will define how I make a life with that person, and I will find a way to make it respected.

Troth is an archaic word, but a very evocative one. As stated in wedding vows, it calls to mind a contract signing in the opulence of fifteenth-century Venice or a contemporary regal recitation in Westminster Cathedral. Simply, troth is defined as belief, faith, loyalty, and trust. With our contemporary society's extreme focus on the "me" in any "we," there is the presupposition of disbelief, unfaithfulness, disloyalty, and betrayal. Even in the act of pledging our troth we are busy positioning ourselves against its possible revocation. Outside of all legal machinations to shore up the promise of such intangible ideas, the pure spirit of their intent remains. The commitment to, and the effort in sustaining, that troth defines a marriage.

Joe and Brad's first visit to my and Jeff's home in Florida held a lot of significance for me. For so many years, I had been the beneficiary of the sense of home that Joe created and shared in each phase of his life. From him, and subsequently from him and Brad together, I learned everything from the nuances of hospitality to how to properly use silver, crystal, and china to their most gracious effect. It was my turn to give back to the ones who gave me so many lessons.

Ultimately, the things I recall of that visit aren't the compliments on the fresh flowers in the guest room or the arrangement of the furniture in the living room. What brought me the greatest satisfaction was an early afternoon when I discovered Brad dozing on the sofa with a book from my bookshelves resting open on his chest. Just outside, Joe lay sleeping in a lounge chair, dappled by the reflection of the canal's refracted light through the leaves of a live oak tree.

The greatest achievement of hospitality is creating a place where loved ones may sleep soundly, secure in every physical and emotional sense. The only such place is home. Happy, I went into the kitchen and started a pot of gumbo.

Brad woke up and wandered into the kitchen. I made him something to drink, and he kept me company while I chopped and diced and sliced the various vegetable components of the stew. We talked of this and that, and then Brad confided that he was very attracted to one of his assistants at the library.

He spoke of the coy courtship of looks and small gestures extended by both of them. He described the sexual tension that ran through the period each day when the assistant appeared for his part-time job. "Of course, it's all mind games," Brad said. "There is no way I'd jeopardize my job or my relationship with Joe for him, no matter how hairy his chest is," he concluded firmly.

"What worries me is that I enjoy the flirting so much," Brad amended. "I've been with Joe for so long, and it's so comfortable, I had forgotten how much fun it can be to just be coy and be courted." I offered that it is okay to look at the menu if you are on a diet, as long as you don't get takeout before you go home. Brad laughed. "You know something," he said, "when you've been married as long as I have, you come to realize that there's still a you underneath all of the commitment crap. It's just that what you want becomes less important than doing anything that might hurt him."

The talk moved to other things, and pretty soon, Brad excused himself to take a shower. I started cleaning shrimp, and Joe came into the kitchen sleepy-eyed and thirsty. I wiped my hands and made him something to drink. As I set it down in front of him, he said, "I'm sorry for just passing out like that. I didn't realize how exhausted I was."

I said, "It makes me very happy that you are comfortable enough in my home to take a nap and know I'll not be offended." As I resumed cleaning the remaining pounds of shrimp, Joe began talking about his job and the stress that went along with it—federal grant application deadlines, budget audits, and people screaming that they were trying to save lives, while he wanted to know how much they spent on gauze pads.

Joe was still talking as I finished with the shrimp and topped them with ice to wait for the last minute to add them to the gumbo. I cleaned up the heads and shells, made myself a drink, and sat down with him at the kitchen table. "You know, the strangest thing has been going on," he said as I lit a cigarette. "There is this little psychiatric social worker down the hall who has been driving me out of my mind."

He went on to tell me that this guy was someone he had met, years ago, before he and Brad became a couple. Then, Joe and this guy had both acknowledged that they were attracted to each other, though they had never followed through with the attraction. Now all these years later, they were working in the same building. Over a period of weeks, it became obvious the old attraction was there, hotter than ever.

"Finally," Joe said, "We met for lunch, just last week, and he asked me if I'd consider having an affair." I ignored the bubbling of the gumbo on the stove; it sounded as though it was cooking too hot. "I want you to know," Joe said as he dropped his voice, "I could have ripped his clothes off and fucked him on the table, right there in the cafeteria, but I told him no."

I just gave him a blank, nonjudgmental look as I got up to stir my gumbo and turn down the heat. Joe cleared his throat and shook himself to get rid of the erotic picture he had no doubt just seen in his head. As much to himself as to me, he said, "Child, I have entirely too much time and effort invested in Brad to try to train another one."

From the stove, I chuckled and said, "Is that right?" Joe planted both hands on the tabletop with a solid, decisive thud. "Besides, I'm getting too damn old to go through all that again. I don't think I could stand to lose Brad," Joe said finally.

Much later, during a Christmas visit, Mom and Dad came home from a shopping excursion and tour of some of Jeff's projects. My mom wandered into the kitchen and opened pot lids on the stove to sniff and see exactly what was cooking. "Jeff introduced us to a friend of ya'll's," Mom said. "Yeah, who?" I responded. "Big. Tall. Italian. Good-looking, umm," she said, her eyes growing wider with each adjective. "What was his name?" I asked. The man she was describing could have been one of a dozen people Jeff and I knew.

"Whoever he is, he said in front of Jeff that you were the best," Dad offered on his way to the refrigerator. Mom nodded and gave me an X-ray mama look. "He said he told you if you ever wanted to leave Jeff, he'd divorce his wife and kids to get with you." It dawned on me who they were talking about. "Aw, Mama, he's so full of shit. He's just a big flirt." Dad retrieved a can of Coke from the refrigerator and gave me an X-ray daddy look, before he took his soda and went into the living room.

"Jeff didn't think he was too funny," Mom challenged. "Jeff knows he ain't got nothing to worry about," I snorted. Mom folded her arms across her bosom and said, "Well, I certainly hope not." While I found her assessment of my desirability based on who I attracted flattering, I found her defensiveness on Jeff's behalf heartwarming.

My mom knows me from way back. She certainly knows what I'm capable of, but she doesn't get to see me on a regular basis. Holidays are a time for best behavior, but every day, nowadays, I'm steady as a rock. The truth of the matter is, the possibility of such an affair had been insinuated, mutually enjoyed as a possibility, and mutually dismissed as ever becoming a reality.

"Mama, honey, if there was no Jeff, you couldn't get me off that man with a crowbar. Do you think I give a damn about his wife and kids?" I paused for effect and watched her eye me carefully. "Well, the truth is, I love Jeff and I'd rather cut myself than hurt him. I'm amazed you don't see that," I said. Mom unfolded her arms and extended them to hug me, "Of course, I see that. You just like to talk ugly." I stepped into her hug and she whispered, "I'd be tempted myself, with that one."

They say human beings aren't born craving either sugar or salt. Once tasted, however, the desire forms and never goes away. In any marriage, there is both. As individuals, the elemental rawness of individuality contains our notions of our own attractiveness, desirability, and personal prowess. As coupled creatures, we experience a combined sweetness in the affirmation of those self-perceptions. As with anything else, the balance between the two sustains mutual attraction and makes commitment concrete.

Heterosexuals are quick to claim that gay people are faithless, hedonistic, primitive creatures incapable of constraining an unbridled sexual urge to mount anything and hump it. Oddly, they don't see the same behavior in themselves or their presidents. Some gay people do buy into that identity for themselves, having surrendered to the notion that they are incapable of commitment, so they might as well have a good time.

Such assessments of our own and other's personal behavior are unfair. Human beings, gay and straight, are a perverse species, impossible to categorize beyond prejudice or generalization. Ample evidence, throughout time, shows that human beings do require companionship and deep emotional connection. The current vogue for serial commitment with numerous partners isn't even a new thing, in gay or straight relationships. Individuals at the extreme ends of levels of wealth, education, and social standing have always enjoyed the latitude to mate and part on a whim.

In the search for another in whom to invest our beliefs, faith, loyalty, and trust, we negotiate a series of complex qualifications and negotiations that seemingly never end. In our deepest commitment to another person is ceaseless scrutiny, assessment, and accommodation. Marriages wither and die when that process stops. When a couple begins to rely simply on a kind of emotional shorthand to maintain their relationship, it is essentially dead. The investment yields no further returns. However, in genuine communication and perpetual adjustment is great endurance.

Three years ago, it became increasingly apparent to Joe that he had hit a glass ceiling in his profession. The only way to break past it to higher levels of challenge and income was to gain more professional credibility through education. He took on the enormous task of going for his MBA while working full-time.

In the effort needed to obtain this degree, Joe's whole life became highly compartmentalized. The effects on his relationship with Brad were lessened by Brad's recognition of what the results of Joe's decreased time and involvement in the home would mean for both of them in the long run. The importance of that supportiveness became underscored as other people in Joe's MBA program began to experience marital difficulties, even to the point of formal separation. Under outside stress and in the light of personal aspirations, couples often see the hairline fractures in their relationships become fully realized cracks.

Joe was very successful in his MBA program, so much so that he was offered a scholarship and research position to enable him to resign his full-time job to go on to pursue his doctorate. Joe and Brad talked it over and mutually agreed that Joe should continue.

This agreement was by no means easy to accept or implement. The university that extended this offer was located more than two hours away. In essence, Joe would have to live there during the week and only come home on weekends. Having honestly discussed the impact that would have on their marriage, they mutually agreed to change their entire lives to accommodate the effort. Joe accepted the university's offer, Brad put in for a transfer, and they put their house on the market with the intention that, when it sold, Brad would move up to join Joe.

The entire first year of this agreement proved to be a nightmare. Brad did receive a transfer, but it now required him to commute more than hour each way to work. They got three offers on the house, two of which fell through. The third offer on the house was so promising, Joe came home and began to pack up all their belongings in anticipation of an early spring closing. That contract fell through as well.

As all of this was going on, Joe was excelling in his course work but was profoundly unhappy with his job. The stresses of a demanding course load combined with an unpleasant work experience were unbearable. Joe found that if he resigned from the job, his scholarship would be revoked. Literally, the solution to the problem would require throwing the baby out with the bathwater.

Frustrated, jerked around, increasingly alienated from each other by distance and school- and work-related demands, Joe and Brad sat down to discuss what they were going to do. There seemed to be no simple solution, until Brad stepped up to the plate. Demonstrating a remarkable commitment to both Joe and their marriage he said, "This is important. I make enough money to support both of us and pay our bills. We'll bite the bullet for the short term while you get your doctorate. Quit that fucking job and concentrate on school. We'll stay right where we're at and manage." It worked.

Certain times in a couple's life require that one person navigates and one person steers. No role, be it social, emotional, financial, or sexual, is engraved in stone. Life throws you curves and opportunities. Individually you grow. For a marriage to be successful, the sense of faithfulness has to include and encourage more than physical fidelity. It requires loyalty to each other's dreams.

As I worked doggedly to finish this book, I became unemployed, as the company I worked for reassessed its whole structure and location. Obviously, I have to work. I have a car payment, a mortgage, and the concomitant insurance costs to keep it all secure. While efforts such as this book are a growing priority in my life, at this time, the effort expended doesn't solely support the result, or vice versa.

I realized, despite my momentary financial panic, that I had a real opportunity at midlife to redefine my goals, my career, and my ambitions. For the majority of my working life, I had taken a series of jobs to which I was only committed in the sense of rightfully earning my paycheck. Few, if any of them, fired my imagination for an extended period of time. Work was something I did to pay for my life; it wasn't my life.

Jeff, on the other hand, has a career to which he has given much care and consideration. Although his work, at times, drives him crazy, he loves what he does. The measure of his success lies as much in his grasping the nuances of the corporate environment as in his understanding those specific to his immediate goals. Jeff is good at what he does. I am proud of him.

Although together we have a comfortable life, to rely solely on either of our incomes isn't a possibility. I was in a quandary. I didn't simply want to get another job just to feed the cash-devouring machinery of our lives. Neither could I afford to simply invest all my time in my creative endeavors.

Jeff has seen me unhappy, but dedicated, for many years. He encouraged me to take stock of what I really liked to do and how much I needed to do it in order to make the money we needed to fuel our life together. He gave me the latitude to find a creative solution to my diverse needs and ambitions. He respects me enough to know my responsibilities to us, to him, and to myself.

Predictably, even in the construction and evolution of my marriage, I have followed an aspect of Joe's life that preceded my own situation. For who we are and where we are from, we have managed to create lives that are remarkably rich, with partners who are incredibly dedicated to us and to the maintenance of a marriage. Allowing even for kismet, karma, and reincarnation, like does attract like. The gift is finding each other. The task is staying together.

In the need for intimacy, security, and love, gay people are no different from any other human beings. The validity of gay marriage, in whatever form it takes, cannot be made more right by any society's notions of legality. Nor can it be stunted by any society's brutal disregard of its reality in fact. Homosexuality and marriage is less a matter of gender and genital preference than it is a matter of where you place your heart and to whom you pledge your troth.

Afterword

The sun at noon provides the clearest light. Life at middle age reveals a broad view of the landscape of our personal history. Prior to that point, our view of ourselves is colored by the rosiness of our expectations and the freshness of new eyes seeing new things. On the other side of middle age, the view is colored by the golden glow of realized dreams, the gray skies of regret, and the purplish shadows of the promise of rest.

As presumptuous as it is to attempt a memoir at middle age, it has been personally instructive. A very dear friend of mine said, on reading the early drafts of this book, "Everyone should be forced to write a memoir—it is a humbling experience." She was more than correct; she was prescient.

I was perhaps less conniving and self-absorbed than I make myself out to be. Joe was, perhaps, less noble and wise than I've painted him. Certainly, even an honest attempt to sort out the feelings and experiences of the difficult craft of living sharpens some edges and dulls others. The truth lies on the working edge.

I look in the mirror and the infrequent photograph hardly recognizing myself sometimes. I see so many others looking back at me. Genetics carve this line, lost ones, that, and living ones, another. I regret the loss of earlier beauty and get in line for the unconsoling compliment of having "character."

I still dress inappropriately for my age and stubbornly refuse to let go of the boy on the beach from so long ago. My surfboard gathers dust in the garage, while I light another cigarette, pour myself a drink, and remember the sun on my back, the salt on my shoulders, and the sudden solidity of speed in the waves beneath my feet.

Joe laughs in the comfort of having a body that still works and doesn't betray the physical ambitions of his age. I have learned the humor and appreciation in that from him. He's still teaching and

I'm still learning. Despite a certain sense of loss for what was, Joe manages to inspire so much enthusiasm for what is just now coming to be.

Life is both salt and sugar. Having tasted both, I'm craving more. At this brief moment of stillness in the swirl of being, I see my life and Joe's in a period of such hard-won richness. In the larger world, so much violence has been perpetrated against gay people, such high costs paid to earn me the freedom to pontificate on my minor queer view of the world.

For all of those men, hunted, hanged, castrated, committed to insane asylums, beaten and robbed and raped, who went before Joe and me, I acknowledge my debt and my gratitude for the relative openness with which we live our lives. In looking ahead, the presumption on my part and Joe's is that we will have somehow contributed to the effort of defining and advancing an identity for the queer young'uns coming along behind us.

I laugh at the whole concept that gay people can't breed, so they have to recruit. That's like inviting someone to a party that serves shit sandwiches and finds cruel humor in playing pin the tail on the guests. The ignorance of the idea speaks for itself. But what I will say to any child, adolescent, or adult who asks is that I wouldn't trade a fucking minute of this gay life. It's been, and probably will continue to be, a hell of a ride.

I am a lucky man. I've managed to find and keep a great deal of love in my life, despite my often obstinate nature directing me only to do things my way. Hopefully, I've earned some respect in that unwillingness to compromise my way of looking at things. Hopefully, it's given me the stones to keep going ahead with my life as I see fit.

There are few illusions I haven't had crushed. It's a certainty that hard times, difficult times, and grief will come again. I'm not scared of that. As long as I have the benefit of following along behind my mentor, I will be prepared for anything that comes. He's shown me how to love somebody, how to laugh, how to grieve, and how to get well and go on.

Now, I look for Joe's broad back as he takes such long strides into the future, hungrily harvesting wisdom and wonder along the way. I look back, even as I try to match his strides, for the gay people who follow behind me. Damn the darkness and the doubt, come out and follow behind us in your own way.

I leave all my readers, gay and straight alike, affirming my concurrence with Saint Augustine, who summed up a lifetime of experience, belief, and wisdom with the simple directive, "Love God and do what you will."

Suggested Reading

Following is a sampling of books that have contributed greatly to the formation of the ideas and attitudes that form this book. It is an eclectic list that includes both straight and gay authors. Although the list is by no means exclusive, it does represent my idea of a jumping-off place for social, philosophical, historical, psychological, and literary thinking that should contribute to the education of an enlightened, informed gay identity.

BIOGRAPHY/MEMOIR

Angelou, Maya (1997). *I Know Why the Caged Bird Sings.* New York: Bantam.

Bragg, Rick (1998). *All Over but the Shoutin'.* New York: Pantheon.

Brown, Rita Mae (1983). *Rubyfruit Jungle.* New York: Bantam.

Dillar, Gavin G. (1998). *In the Flesh: Undress for Success.* New York: Barricade Books.

Doty, Mark (1997). *Heaven's Coast: A Memoir.* New York: HarperCollins.

Eribon, Didier (1991). *Michel Foucault.* Betsy Wing, Trans. Cambridge, MA: Harvard University Press.

Gooch, Brad (1993). *City Poet: The Life and Times of Frank O'Hara.* New York: Knopf.

Monk, Ray (1990). *Ludwig Wittgenstein: The Duty of Genius.* New York: Penguin Books.

Reid, John (1993). *The Best Little Boy in the World.* New York: Ballantine.

Rivers, Larry with Harvey Weinstein (1992). *What Did I Do?* New York: Harper-Collins.

Tobias, Andrew (1998). *The Best Little Boy in the World Grows Up.* New York: Random House.

Vidal, Gore (1995). *Palimpsest: A Memoir.* New York: Random House.

GAY SOCIAL ISSUES

Bawer, Bruce (1996). *Beyond Queer.* New York: The Free Press.

Browning, Frank (1998). *Culture of Desire: Paradox and Peversity in Gay Lives Today.* New York: Crown Publishing Group.

Shilts, Randy (1993). *And the Band Played On: Politics, People, and the AIDS Epidemic.* New York: Viking Penguin.

Shilts, Randy (1994). *Conduct Unbecoming: Gays and Lesbians in the U.S. Military.* New York: Fawcett.

Shilts, Randy (1998). *Conduct Unbecoming: Gays and Lesbians in the U.S. Military—Vietnam to the Persian Gulf.* Upland, PA: DIANE Publishing Company.

Vaid, Urvashi (1995). *Virtual Equality: The Mainstreaming of Gay and Lesbian Liberation.* New York: Doubleday.

Zeeland, Steven (1995). *Sailors and Sexual Identity: Crossing the Line Between "Straight" and "Gay" in the U.S. Navy.* Binghamton, NY: The Haworth Press, Inc.

HISTORY

Burg, Barry Richard (1995). *Sodomy and the Pirate Tradition: English Sea Rovers in the Seventeenth Century Caribbean,* Second Revised Edition (Original title: *Sodomy and the Perception of Evil).* New York: New York University Press.

Dover, Kenneth J. (1997). *Greek Homosexuality,* Reprint Edition. New York: Fine Communications.

Green, Peter (1996). *Alexander of Macedon, 356-323 B.C. A Historial Perspective.* Berkeley, CA: University of California Press.

Lowry, Thomas P. (1994). *The Story the Soldiers Wouldn't Tell: Sex in the Civil War.* Mechanicsburg, PA: Stackpole.

Spencer, Colin (1995). *Homsexuality in History.* New York: Harcourt Brace.

PHILOSOPHY

Foucault, Michel (1988). *Care of the Self.* New York: Random House.

Foucault, Michel (1990). *The History of Sexuality: An Introduction.* New York: Vintage Books.

Foucault, Michel (1990). *The Use of Pleasure: The History of Sexuality.* New York: Vintage Books.

Nietzche, Friedrich Wilhelm (1977). *The Portable Nietzche.* Walter Kaufman, Editor. New York: Penguin Books.

Plato (1965). *Works of Plato.* Irwin Edman, Editor; Benjamin E. Jowett, Translator. New York: McGraw-Hill.

Saint Augustine (1991). *Confessions.* Henry Chadwick, Translator. Oxford: Oxford University Press.

Wittgenstein, Ludwig (1967). *Wittgenstein: Lectures and Conversations on Aesthetics, Psychology and Religious Belief.* Cyril Barrett, Editor. Berkeley, CA: University of California Press.

Wittgenstein, Ludwig (1994). *Tractatus Logico-Philosophicus.* English Translation. B. F. McGuiness, Editor; D. F. Pears, Translator. New York: Routledge.

PSYCHOLOGY

Macey, David (1988). *Lacan in Contexts.* New York: Verso.
Rank, Otto (1975). *Art and Artist: Creative Urge and Personality Development.* Charles Francis Atkinson, Translator. New York: Agathon Press.
Roland, Alan (Ed.) (1978). *Psychoanalysis, Creativity, and Literature: A French-American Inquiry.* New York: Columbia University Press.
Spitz, Ellen Handler (1985). *Art and Psyche: A Study of Psychoanalysis and Aesthetics.* New Haven, CT: Yale University Press.
Weinstock, Nicholas (1998). *The Secret Love of Sons.* New York: Putnam Publishing Group.

RELIGION

Boswell, John (1995). *Same-Sex Unions in Premodern Europe.* New York: Random House.
Boswell, John (1981). *Christianity, Social Tolerance, and Homosexuality: Gay People in Western Europe from the Beginning of the Christian Era to the Fourteenth Century.* Chicago, IL: University of Chicago Press.
Bouldrey, Brian (1996). *Wrestling with the Angel: Faith and Religion in the Lives of Gay Men.* New York: Berkley Publishing.
The New English Bible, Oxford Edition.
Sullivan, Andrew (1998). *Love Undetectable.* New York: Knopf.

FICTION

There is no bad "gay" fiction, in the sense that each and every individual gay author reveals some facet of gay identity. Likewise, each gay character created by a straight writer is an accomplishment that identifies our enemies or allies in the effort to bring gay people into the direct consciousness of all people.

I have personal favorites among all such authors. The following list is only a fraction of those who create the mirror for gay identity that helps us recognize and define ourselves. It is important to read these authors, but it is more important *to read.* Exhaustively, tirelessly experience the education and entertainment provided for you by those people who have had the courage to create a gay world for everyone to wander in.

Specifically, but not exclusively:

Laura Argiri
Dorothy Allison
William Baldwin
Harold Brodkey
Rita Mae Brown
Jean Cocteau

Michael Cunningham
Jean Genet
Brad Gooch
Allan Gurganus
Andrew Holleran
Alan Hollinghurst

Larry Kramer
David Leavitt
Paul Lisicky
Thomas Mann
Colleen McCullough
Gordon Mereick
Paul Monette
Anais Nin

Felice Picano
Reynolds Price
Mary Renault
Anne Rice
Gore Vidal
Patricia Nell Warren
Edmund White
Frank Yerby